# Prescription and
# Non-prescription Drugs

# Prescription and Non-prescription Drugs

Paul Ruschmann, J.D.

SERIES CONSULTING EDITOR
Alan Marzilli, M.A., J.D.

CHELSEA HOUSE
PUBLISHERS
An imprint of Infobase Publishing

**Prescription and Non-prescription Drugs**

Copyright © 2007 by Infobase Publishing

Chelsea House
An imprint of Infobase Publishing
132 West 31st Street
New York NY 10001

**Library of Congress Cataloging-in-Publication Data**

Ruschmann, Paul.
  Prescription and non-prescription drugs / Paul Ruschmann.
    p. cm. — (Point/counterpoint)
  Includes bibliographical references and index.
  ISBN-13: 978-0-7910-9552-2 (hardcover)
  ISBN-10: 0-7910-9552-5 (hardcover)
  1. Drugs—Law and legislation—United States. 2. Pharmacy—Law and legislation—United States. I. Title. II. Series.

  KF3885.R87 2007
  344.7304'233—dc22                                    2007015488

Chelsea House books are available at special discounts when purchased in bulk quantities for businesses, associations, institutions, or sales promotions. Please call our Special Sales Department in New York at (212) 967-8800 or (800) 322-8755.

You can find Chelsea House on the World Wide Web at
http://www.chelseahouse.com

Series design by Keith Trego
Cover design by Keith Trego and Joo Young An

Printed in the United States of America

Bang  NMSG 10 9 8 7 6 5 4 3 2 1

This book is printed on acid-free paper.

All links and Web addresses were checked and verified to be correct at the time of publication. Because of the dynamic nature of the Web, some addresses and links may have changed since publication and may no longer be valid.

# CONTENTS

# Foreword

Alan Marzilli, M.A., J.D.
Washington, D.C.

The debates presented in POINT/COUNTERPOINT are among the most interesting and controversial in contemporary American society, but studying them is more than an academic activity. They affect every citizen; they are the issues that today's leaders debate and tomorrow's will decide. The reader may one day play a central role in resolving them.

Why study both sides of the debate? It's possible that the reader will not yet have formed any opinion at all on the subject of this volume—but this is unlikely. It is more likely that the reader will already hold an opinion, probably a strong one, and very probably one formed without full exposure to the arguments of the other side. It is rare to hear an argument presented in a balanced way, and it is easy to form an opinion on too little information; these books will help to fill in the informational gaps that can never be avoided. More important, though, is the practical function of the series: Skillful argumentation requires a thorough knowledge of *both* sides—though there are seldom only two, and only by knowing what an opponent is likely to assert can one form an articulate response.

Perhaps more important is that listening to the other side sometimes helps one to see an opponent's arguments in a more human way. For example, Sister Helen Prejean, one of the nation's most visible opponents of capital punishment, has been deeply affected by her interactions with the families of murder victims. Seeing the families' grief and pain, she understands much better why people support the death penalty, and she is able to carry out her advocacy with a greater sensitivity to the needs and beliefs of those who do not agree with her. Her relativism, in turn, lends credibility to her work. Dismissing the other side of the argument as totally without merit can be too easy—it is far more useful to understand the nature of the controversy and the reasons *why* the issue defies resolution.

The most controversial issues of all are often those that center on a constitutional right. The Bill of Rights—the first ten amendments to the U.S. Constitution—spells out some of the most fundamental rights that distinguish the governmental system of the United States from those that allow fewer (or other) freedoms. But the sparsely worded document is open to interpretation, and clauses of only a few words are often at the heart of national debates. The Bill of Rights was meant to protect individual liberties; but the needs of some individuals clash with those of society as a whole, and when this happens someone has to decide where to draw the line. Thus the Constitution becomes a battleground between the rights of individuals to do as they please and the responsibility of the government to protect its citizens. The First Amendment's guarantee of "freedom of speech," for example, leads to a number of difficult questions. Some forms of expression, such as burning an American flag, lead to public outrage—but nevertheless are said to be protected by the First Amendment. Other types of expression that most people find objectionable, such as sexually explicit material involving children, are not protected because they are considered harmful. The question is not only where to draw the line, but how to do this without infringing on the personal liberties on which the United States was built.

The Bill of Rights raises many other questions about individual rights and the societal "good." Is a prayer before a high school football game an "establishment of religion" prohibited by the First Amendment? Does the Second Amendment's promise of "the right to bear arms" include concealed handguns? Is stopping and frisking someone standing on a corner known to be frequented by drug dealers a form of "unreasonable search and seizure" in violation of the Fourth Amendment? Although the nine-member U.S. Supreme Court has the ultimate authority in interpreting the Constitution, its answers do not always satisfy the public. When a group of nine people—sometimes by a five-to-four vote—makes a decision that affects the lives of hundreds of millions, public outcry can be expected. And the composition of the Court does change over time, so even a landmark decision is not guaranteed to stand forever. The limits of constitutional protection are always in flux.

These issues make headlines, divide courts, and decide elections. They are the questions most worthy of national debate, and this series aims to cover them as thoroughly as possible. Each volume sets out some of the key arguments surrounding a particular issue, even some views that most people consider extreme or radical—but presents a balanced perspective on the issue. Excerpts from the relevant laws and judicial opinions and references to central concepts, source material, and advocacy groups help the reader to explore the issues even further and to read "the letter of the law" just as the legislatures and the courts have established it.

It may seem that some debates—such as those over capital punishment and abortion, debates with a strong moral component—will never be resolved. But American history offers numerous examples of controversies that once seemed insurmountable but now are effectively settled, even if only on the surface. Abolitionists met with widespread resistance to their efforts to end slavery, and the controversy over that issue threatened to cleave the nation in two; but today public debate over the merits of slavery would be unthinkable, though racial inequalities still plague the nation. Similarly unthinkable at one time was suffrage for women and minorities, but this is now a matter of course. Distributing information about contraception once was a crime. Societies change, and attitudes change, and new questions of social justice are raised constantly while the old ones fade into irrelevancy.

Whatever the root of the controversy, the books in POINT/ COUNTERPOINT seek to explain to the reader the origins of the debate, the current state of the law, and the arguments on both sides. The goal of the series is to inform the reader about the issues facing not only American politicians, but all of the nation's citizens, and to encourage the reader to become more actively involved in resolving these debates, as a voter, a concerned citizen, a journalist, an activist, or an elected official. Democracy is based on education, and every voice counts—so every opinion must be an informed one.

———————•————————•————————•———

This volume examines how the U.S. government regulates the prescription and non-prescription drugs that we use to relieve pain, fight infections, and control various medical conditions. Modern medications have helped increase life expectancies, with millions relying on certain medications to stay alive or maintain their day-to-day functioning. At the same time, all of the medications that we are taking support a multibillion dollar industry that is constantly trying to bring new drugs to the marketplace. We cannot turn on the television without hearing a commercial for a prescription drug. Standing between the manufacturers and the public is the U.S. Food and Drug Administration, which regulates the safety and effectiveness of medications, and Congress, which can pass laws affecting the manufacture, sale, and use of medications.

With prescription drug costs increasing and several high-profile drugs having been found to be harmful, the regulation of the pharmaceutical industry is a hot topic. Some of the competing interests in the debate include the pharmaceutical industry, the medical profession, patients' groups, older Americans, and organizations devoted to consumer protections. Sometimes these groups are allies, while at other times they are on different sides of the debate. Some of the controversial issues include balancing the need for drugs to get to market quickly against the need to ensure that they are safe, making prescription drugs more affordable, and regulating the way that drugs are marketed.

# Drug Regulation in America

On September 30, 2004, Merck & Co. withdrew from the market a prescription pain-relief drug called Vioxx because studies indicated an increased risk of heart attacks in patients who took high dosages for a long period of time. Some believe that the drug was responsible for 50,000 or more deaths. The Vioxx recall was said to be the biggest product recall in prescription drug history.

Even after it withdrew the drug, Merck continued to defend it. Still, some people within the medical community maintain that the company had known for years about Vioxx's side effects but aggressively marketed it anyway. The U.S. Food and Drug Administration (FDA), which approved Vioxx in 1999, also came under fire for not having reacted sooner to evidence that the drug was potentially deadly. Some called the government's handling of Vioxx a "regulatory failure."

Even if Vioxx never returns to the market, the repercussions are likely to be felt for years. Critics believe that drugs such as Vioxx are allowed on the market because the FDA has been weakened by the wealth and influence of drug companies. But defenders of drug companies insist that, despite pharmaceutical side effects, new drugs have helped millions of Americans live longer and fuller lives; they add that the real problem is not a handful of drugs with serious side effects, but heavy-handed regulations that keep life-saving medications away from patients.

## A Wide-Open Market for Drugs

Thousands of years ago, human beings discovered that certain substances could heal the human body or relieve pain. In some ancient societies, those who practiced medicine left behind written compilations detailing the substances they used to treat the sick. Medical historian Dr. Roderick McGrew describes one such compilation, which was discovered in what is now Iraq:

> The tablets refer to vegetable drugs, 150 mineral drugs, and a variety of substances with medical uses, including alcoholic drinks, fats and oils, animal parts and milk, and honey and wax. Instructions for compounding and administering drugs show familiarity with some chemical principles and complex refining procedures.[1]

The so-called pharmaceutical tradition also had a foothold in ancient Greece and Rome; however, after the Roman Empire fell, that tradition virtually disappeared in Western Europe. By medieval times, medical knowledge could best be described as primitive. Medicine and pharmacology made little progress during the centuries that followed.

Medical journalist Philip Hilts, who wrote a history of the federal FDA, commented on the state of medicine two centuries ago:

**Dr. Peter S. Kim (left), president of Merck's research labs, and Raymond V. Gilmartin, chairman, president, and CEO of Merck, announce the company's voluntary withdrawal of Vioxx on September 30, 2004. Vioxx is a medication for the treatment of arthritis and acute pain.**

In Egypt four thousand years earlier, life expectancy was about thirty-six years. At the opening of the nineteenth century, it was about thirty-seven years. It was for want of a method, a tool to pry open the secrets of health and disease, and by which remedies could be tested reliably, that the essential mysteries had gone unsolved.[2]

Only a few of the medical compounds used at the time were beneficial. They included morphine and its derivatives to relieve pain; digitalis leaf, from the foxglove plant, for heart disease; aspirin, from willow bark, for fever and inflammation; and a handful of others. By one estimate, a patient had only a fifty-fifty chance of benefiting from a visit to a doctor's office.

But scientists at this time were about to take the first steps toward developing better medicines. McGrew observed that their discoveries "made it possible to standardize quality, eliminate impurities, make dosages more accurate, and achieve a more discriminating understanding of drugs' effects."[3] Companies whose names are recognizable today—such as Bristol-Meyers Squibb, Eli Lilly, Parke-Davis and Company, and Merck—entered the business of manufacturing drugs.

## Patent Medicines, the "Muckrakers," and the Pure Food and Drug Act

The American approach to medication followed the English model, in which there was little regulation. Although doctors and pharmacists took steps to organize themselves, they lacked the power to rid their fields of dishonest and incompetent practitioners. Some, however, campaigned for higher standards for their members and for a crackdown on "patent medicines" whose ingredients—which included alcohol and even addictive drugs—were kept a secret. They also fought the widespread practice of "self-medication," and campaigned to rid the market of ineffective over-the-counter products. Their efforts ran into opposition from unethical practitioners who feared losing their livelihood; from the patent-medicine industry; and from business interests who believed that the government should not interfere with the free market.

At the time, the federal government took the approach of *caveat emptor*, Latin for "let the buyer beware." In other words, it was up to consumers to fend for themselves. What little government regulation there was existed only at the state level. Legal experts believed that the Constitution gave the federal government power over narrowly defined areas—such as maintaining a military and running the post office—and left the states in charge of passing public health and safety laws.

The late nineteenth century was a time of widespread corruption, which extended to companies that made food and medicine. Because the government did not take action, many Americans joined protest movements that demanded safer food and drugs. At the turn of the twentieth century, journalists and authors known as "muckrakers" were practicing what is today called investigative journalism. Their writing exposed the abusive practices of the government and corporations, and demanded reform. A series of exposés of the food industry, climaxing with

## The Pure Food and Drug Act of 1906

On June 6, 1906, President Theodore Roosevelt signed the Pure Food and Drug Act [34 Stat. 584; 59th Congress, Chapter 3915], the first major federal law that regulated drugs.

Sections 1 and 2 of the act provided that it would be a misdemeanor to manufacture, sell, or import adulterated food or drugs or to transport such goods across state lines.

Sections 3 through 5 dealt with enforcement of the act and provided for the following:

(1) It required the Department of the Treasury, the Department of Agriculture, and the Department of Labor to adopt rules governing the collection and examination of products.

(2) It directed the Bureau of Chemistry in the Department of Agriculture to examine products and, if it discovered a possible violation, to notify the U.S. attorney whose office had jurisdiction over that violation.

(3) It directed a U.S. attorney who had been notified of a violation to start criminal proceedings against the alleged violator.

In its original form, the act did not create an agency charged with enforcing its provisions. It was not until 1927 that Congress created the Food, Drug and Insecticide Administration, which was later renamed the Food and Drug Administration.

Section 6 defined which products were covered by the act. The term "drug" included those medicines and preparations that were recognized in the U.S. Pharmacopoeia or National Formulary, as well as any substance or mixture of substances that was used or intended to be used to cure, mitigate, or prevent disease in either humans or animals.

the publication of Upton Sinclair's novel *The Jungle* (describing unhealthy practices in the meat-packing industry), moved Congress to pass the Pure Food and Drug Act of 1906.

The act was relatively weak. Penalties were light, there were numerous loopholes, and, most importantly, it did not actually require that drugs be safe. Nevertheless, the act opened the door for federal regulation of the drug industry. Philip Hilts explains:

Section 7 defined a drug as "adulterated" if it differed from the standard of strength, quality, or purity set out in the U.S. Pharmacopoeia or National Formulary, and that difference was not plainly disclosed to the consumer; or if its strength or purity was below the professed standard or quality under which it was sold.

Section 8 defined a drug as "misbranded" if its package or label either contained a false or misleading statement about it, or falsely represented that it was made in a different state or country than the one where it was actually made. It also provided that a drug was misbranded if:

(1) It was an imitation of, or offered for sale under the name of, another drug;
(2) Its original contents were removed and replaced with something else; or
(3) Its package failed to disclose the presence and amount of certain ingredients, including alcohol, morphine, opium, cocaine, heroin, chloroform, or cannabis (the active ingredient in marijuana).

Section 9 provided that a retailer who sold a product that was guaranteed pure by the manufacturer or wholesaler could not be prosecuted for violating the act.

Section 10 authorized the government to start a legal proceeding against an allegedly adulterated or misbranded product. In such a proceeding, the product itself was the "defendant." A court that found a product adulterated or misbranded could either destroy it or sell it.

Section 11 authorized the government to stop the importation of adulterated or misbranded products, products that were illegal in the United States or in the country where they originated, or products that were "otherwise dangerous to the people of the United States."

Section 13 provided that the act would take effect January 1, 1907.

Though it was not understood at the time, the change in policy that came with this law was a fundamental one. It was an assertion that it was the job of the government to protect citizens from some kinds of commerce rather than just to protect commerce. It was recognition that business most often had the means to take care of itself regarding government policy, but the average citizen did not. It acknowledged that there are instances, such as the ensuring of a supply of safe and wholesome food and medicine for the nation, in which the government must protect citizens against business. It would not be an easy principle to enforce.[4]

## The "Massengill Massacre" and Its Aftermath

During the 1930s, a bill that would strengthen the Pure Food and Drug Act languished in Congress because the drug industry objected to stronger regulation. Then, however, a disaster known as the "Massengill Massacre" focused attention on the weakness of existing drug laws and forced lawmakers to act.

At the time, scientists had developed "sulfa" drugs, which could kill bacterial infections such as strep throat and treat sexually transmitted diseases. The Massengill Company of Bristol, Tennessee, manufactured a drug called sulfanilamide. It produced the drug in pill form, but company salesmen told management that doctors and patients preferred a better-tasting version that could be taken in liquid form.

If Massengill could produce a liquid form of the drug, it would enjoy a substantial advantage over its competitors. By a process of trial and error, the company's chief chemist discovered that a liquid version could be made using diethylene glycol, a slightly sweet but mostly tasteless fluid. Massengill marketed it under the name Elixir Sulfanilamide.

What the company did not realize was that diethylene glycol was highly toxic when taken by humans. Soon after Elixir Sulfanilamide went on the market, doctors reported to the American Medical Association and the FDA that their patients had died after taking it. Walter Campbell, the head of the FDA, discovered that he had little power to prosecute Massengill. The Pure Food and Drug Act outlawed

In 1927, Congress created what is now known as the Food and Drug Administration. The FDA today is part of the U.S. Department of Health and Human Services.

## Pharmacy Embraces Science: The Food, Drug and Cosmetic Act of 1938

During the 1930s, public-health advocates argued that the Pure Food and Drug Act had become outdated, but the business community used its influence to block a bill that would strengthen the original law. Then came the "Massengill Massacre," in which more than 100 people died after taking an anti-infection drug

misleading statements on product labels, but not dangerous drugs, per se. Campbell, however, discovered a legal technicality—Massengill had wrongly used the word "elixir," a term that refers to a liquid containing alcohol—and on that basis went ahead with an investigation. FDA investigators tracked down most of the Elixir Sulfanilamide that was still on the market. They also questioned Massengill's president, who admitted that his company had not conducted safety tests before shipping the elixir, but pointed out that the law required no such tests.

At least 107 people, most of them children, died after taking Elixir Sulfanilamide. Massengill was fined $26,000 for mislabeling; at the time, that was the largest fine ever levied by the FDA.

In the wake of the Massengill Massacre, many Americans expressed their support for stronger drug laws. Lawmakers not only passed the bill that had been stalled in Congress but also added an important requirement: manufacturers had to conduct safety tests and submit the results to the FDA before marketing a new drug.

On June 15, 1938, President Franklin D. Roosevelt signed the Food, Drug and Cosmetic Act, 52 Stat. 1040, 75th Congress, Chapter 675. In addition to requiring evidence that a drug was safe, the act outlawed false health claims about drugs, authorized federal inspection of factories, and required that drugs be labeled with adequate directions so that they could be used safely.

There were two notable shortcomings in the 1938 act, however: drugs that were already on the market could continue to be sold, whether or not they were safe, and there was no requirement that new drugs be *effective* as well as safe.

that also contained a deadly poison. Bowing to the public outcry that followed, Congress passed the Food, Drug and Cosmetic Act of 1938.

The intent of the 1938 act was to protect Americans from unsafe drugs. It gave the FDA the power to prevent a new drug from coming onto the market, and required scientific evidence, as opposed to assurances from the manufacturer or the opinions of doctors, to establish the safety of new drugs. According to Philip Hilts, "the competitive edge shifted from cheapness and advertising aggressiveness to research and testing of drugs."[5] The act helped to usher in the prescription system, under which the most potent drugs were given to a patient only after he or she consulted a doctor who concluded that the drug was appropriate.

In the years that followed, scientists went on the offensive, looking for drugs that could cure deadly diseases. Drug companies mass-produced substances such as penicillin, which killed disease-causing bacteria. Most patent medicines disappeared from the market, and the pharmaceutical industry came to be dominated by large companies whose products were developed in laboratories.

## The "Safe and Effective" Requirement Becomes Law

During the 1950s, the U.S. pharmaceutical industry developed the form it has today. Drug company researchers discovered a new substance or bought the rights to a discovered substance from a university. The company patented those substances that looked promising, tested them for safety and effectiveness, and submitted the test results to the FDA. Finally, if everything seemed in order, the company marketed the drug. It promoted the product by hiring "detail men" to call on doctors and tell them about new drugs.

Some reformers believed that the government was still not doing enough to keep ineffective drugs off the market or to curb unfair practices such as companies fixing the prices of their drugs. Despite calls for stronger regulations, it again took a drug disaster to pass legislation. A drug called thalidomide was being marketed in Europe as a sleep aid and a remedy for morning sickness in pregnant women, but an FDA regulator held up its introduction in the United States. After it was learned that thousands of babies with deformed limbs had been born to European women who took thalidomide, the American agency drew praise for preventing sale of the drug in the United States.

In an effort to avoid another thalidomide disaster, Congress passed the 1962 Kefauver-Harris Amendments to the Food, Drug and Cosmetic Act. A central provision of that law required the drug manufacturer to provide the FDA with "substantial evidence" that a new drug would live up to the manufacturer's claims about it. "Substantial evidence" meant "evidence consisting of adequate and well-controlled investigations, including clinical investigations, by experts qualified by scientific training and experience to evaluate the effectiveness of the drug involved."[6]

Drug companies were thus required to follow new FDA procedures to establish safety and effectiveness. At the heart of those procedures is the requirement of clinical drug trials, carefully-controlled experiments that measure the effect of a new drug by comparing a group of patients who took it against a second group that took another substance (for example, a placebo—a sugar pill that contains no medication). Philip Hilts observed, "[t]he standard that medicines would be held to now was a seriously scientific one, the first important instance in lawmaking when that was the case."[7]

## Deregulation and Other Challenges

The election of Ronald Reagan in 1980 ushered in an era of "deregulation," when policymakers questioned both the effectiveness of laws that regulated business and the government agencies that enforced them. The FDA was no exception. Conservatives accused the agency of playing politics, being prejudiced against business, and even killing Americans by unreasonably holding up approval of beneficial drugs. They called for further loosening of laws regulating the pharmaceutical industry. Some even proposed that the FDA be abolished.

## The Controlled Substances Act

The Controlled Substances Act, Title 21, §801, and following of the U.S. Code, took effect in 1970. It was part of an overhaul of the nation's narcotics laws. The act's most important feature was a classification system: depending on the danger of abuse or addiction, and the extent to which they are used in medical practice, drugs are assigned to "schedules" with varying levels of regulation.

In assigning drugs to a schedule, Title 21, §811(c) directs the federal government to consider the following:

(1) The drug's actual or relative potential for abuse.
(2) Scientific evidence of its known effect on the human body.
(3) The state of current scientific knowledge of the drug.
(4) Its history and current pattern of abuse.
(5) The scope, duration, and significance of abuse.
(6) What risk, if any, the drug poses to public health.
(7) The risk that users will become physically or psychologically dependent on it.
(8) Whether the drug is used, or is likely to be used, to produce a substance already controlled under the act.

Two federal departments—the Department of Justice and the Department of Health and Human Services, which receives input from the Food and Drug Administration—determine which drugs are added to or removed from the various schedules. The act recognizes the following five schedules:

*Schedule I*: No prescriptions may be written for drugs on this schedule. The category includes cannabis (marijuana and hashish), heroin, Ecstasy, LSD, mescaline, and peyote (though some Native Americans are allowed to use peyote as part of their religious ceremonies).

*Schedule II*: These drugs are available by prescription only. The category includes cocaine, Ritalin, opium, oxycodone (the main ingredient in the pain relievers Percocet and OxyContin), morphine, and amphetamine (a drug that stimulates the central nervous system).

At the same time, Congress passed laws that benefited the pharmaceutical industry. Lawmakers permitted drug companies to buy the discoveries made by taxpayer-funded scientists;

*Schedule III*: Like drugs in Schedule II, these are available by prescription only; however, controls on distribution and on prescription refills are less stringent. The category includes anabolic steroids (compounds that grow and repair human tissue, but are sometimes used by athletes to increase their size and strength), and the pain relievers Vicodin and Tylenol 3.

*Schedule IV*: Controls of drugs in this schedule are similar to those in Schedule III. The category includes tranquilizers such as Xanax, Librium, and Valium, and the sleep aid Ambien.

*Schedule V*: Some drugs in this schedule are available without a prescription. The category includes drugs with small amounts of opium or codeine, such as some cough suppressants.

Some states have added a "Schedule VI" to their drug laws in an effort to control access to certain substances that are not "drugs" in the conventional sense but are nonetheless abused recreationally, especially by young people. The category includes toluene (a chemical found in spray paint) and inhalants such as nitrous oxide, which is found in aerosol cans. Many state and local governments enforce age limits on the sale of these products.

Some argue that classification decisions are driven by politics as much as by public health. Dr. David Musto, a medical historian who teaches at Yale University, observed:

> Establishing actual dangerousness sounds reasonable, but the process had its difficulties. If the dangers of drugs were to be ranked according to deaths linked to their use, tobacco and alcohol [which are not covered by the Controlled Substances Act] would head the list. These substances, however, had powerful economic and political interests behind them and moreover were not part of the public's fear over the drug crisis.*

*David F. Musto, *Drugs in America: A Documentary History*. New York: New York University Press, 2002, p. 260.

extended "patent protection," the exclusive legal right to market a drug; cracked down on the importation of prescription drugs; offered incentives to find treatments for rare diseases; and gave tax breaks to make up for the high cost of developing drugs. They also provided for "fast-track" approval for certain drugs, such as those for treating AIDS and cancer.

Some critics believe that the trend toward deregulation has gone too far. They contend that the FDA has been taken over by the industry that it is supposed to regulate. They further charge that the agency cannot resist pressure to approve new drugs before their safety has been established, and that it also lacks the resources to monitor drugs that have already been approved.

## Narcotics Laws: Another Form of Drug Regulation

For thousands of years, human beings have used drugs to alter their moods. The earliest such drugs were natural substances such as marijuana and coca leaves, or alcoholic beverages. During the nineteenth century, scientists found ways to extract even more powerful drugs. Those new drugs, however, also had more serious side effects, such as addiction and the potential for lethal overdoses. At first, many in the medical profession were unaware of how dangerous certain substances were; for example, when cocaine first appeared, some doctors considered it no more dangerous than coffee. Since regulation barely existed, products containing opium, cocaine, and even heroin were available over the counter.

Once lawmakers realized how addictive some drugs were, they imposed controls over them. Safety was not the only reason for regulation; many Americans objected on religious grounds to "recreational" drug use. A prominent activist of the early twentieth century, the Right Reverend Charles Brent, took a moralistic approach to the use of mood-altering substances:

> Did narcotics have a value other than as a medicine? No: unlike alcohol they had no beverage or caloric value. Should

such substances be permitted for casual use? No: there was no justification, since there was the possibility only of danger in narcotics for nonmedicinal uses. Therefore recreational use of narcotics should be prohibited, their traffic curtailed on a world scale, and a scourge eliminated from the earth.[8]

Unsure whether it had the power to step in, the federal government was slow to regulate narcotics. The first federal law was the Harrison Narcotics Act, which was passed in 1914. Federal regulation was later extended to marijuana and then to stimulants and tranquilizers. In 1970, Congress passed the Controlled Substances Act[9] as part of an overhaul of federal narcotics laws. The act strictly regulates who can manufacture, distribute, and even possess certain drugs.

To some extent, narcotics laws overlap pure food and drug laws. Some drugs—for example, Ritalin, which is used to treat attention deficit disorder—are both controlled substances and available by prescription only. Others are available by prescription only, but are not controlled substances because the risk of abuse is considered low. Still others are controlled substances but not prescription drugs because they have no legally recognized medical use—marijuana use (in most states) is one example—or else the medical profession has abandoned them in favor of safer alternatives.

## Summary

The recall of Vioxx, a drug that has been blamed for thousands of deaths, refocused attention on how well the U.S. government protects citizens from dangerous drugs. A century ago, the science of medicine was primitive and there were virtually no drug laws. Some drugs on the market were harmful and consumers were unaware that they could kill. As people learned that some medicines had deadly side effects, they prevailed upon lawmakers to enact stronger regulations. Today, both prescription and non-prescription drugs must be proven safe and effective before the Food and Drug Administration allows them to be sold.

# Drug Companies' Business Practices Endanger Americans

The twentieth century saw the development of "wonder drugs" that fight infection, relieve pain, and help control conditions such as diabetes. Those same drugs, however, are sometimes harmful or even deadly—far more so than Americans realize. Philip Hilts explains:

> A table of risk put together by Thomas Moore of George Washington University estimates the lifetime chance of being put in the hospital by accidents: severe injury by prescription drugs, 26 in 100; auto accident, 2 in 100; murder, one in 100; commercial air crash, one in 35,000.[10]

Critics believe that the government does not take drug safety seriously enough, and that lax regulation will someday lead to another drug disaster.

## Drug companies' priorities are misplaced.

Jacky Law, a medical journalist, observes that "[t]he human race can survive perfectly well without an endless supply of new drugs but the corporations that produce them can't."[11] To survive, drug companies must develop a "pipeline" of medications and promote them aggressively. In the pharmaceutical industry, a handful of "blockbuster" drugs—the industry's term for drugs that bring in $1 billion or more per year—account for much of its revenue. In 2003, a mere 10 drugs brought in a combined total of $48.3 billion.

However, some "new" drugs are no better than those that were developed years ago. According to Dr. Marcia Angell, the former editor of the *New England Journal of Medicine*, "[b]etween 1998 and 2002, 77 percent of 'new drugs' approved by the FDA were 'me-too' drugs, which were neither innovations (14 percent) nor significant improvements over existing drugs (nine percent)."[12] Some companies have even cut back production of life-saving medications in order to concentrate on highly profitable drugs. Angell observed:

> In 2001, there were serious shortages of many important drugs, including certain anesthetics, antivenins for poisonous snakebites, steroids for premature infants, antidotes for certain drug overdoses, an anticlotting drug for hemophilia, an injectable drug used in cardiac resuscitation, an antibiotic for gonorrhea, a drug to induce labor in childbirth, and vaccines against flu and pneumonia in adults.[13]

## There are too many drugs on the market.

Philip Hilts observes that "[t]oday, 10,000 to 15,000 drugs are on the market, and the World Health Organization considers that a properly equipped pharmacy needs only 350 of them."[14] The flood of new drugs has undermined the doctor's traditional role as a "gatekeeper" who knew how prescription drugs affected the body and protected his or her patients from inappropriate

## The FDA Keeps Thalidomide Off the Market

During the late 1950s, the German company Chemie Grünenthal marketed a drug called thalidomide, a sleeping pill that also promised to relieve morning sickness in pregnant women. At first, it appeared to be an improvement over existing tranquilizers, which some patients found addictive.

Chemie Grünenthal put thalidomide on the market in a number of European countries without having sufficiently tested it. It also appears that company officials ignored evidence that suggested the drug caused nerve damage. Later, even worse side effects appeared: some women who took the drug gave birth to babies with arms and legs that looked like the flippers of a seal. An estimated 10,000 children with serious birth defects were born to mothers who took thalidomide.

Only a handful of the victims were Americans because an FDA medical officer, Frances Oldham Kelsey, kept the drug off the market. Richardson-Merrill, which owned the U.S. rights to thalidomide, asked the FDA to approve its sale. Agency officials handed the application to Kelsey to evaluate. Under the existing laws at the time, Richardson-Merrill could market the drug unless the FDA objected within 60 days. Kelsey did object because Richardson-Merrill's application caused her to be concerned that patients who took thalidomide might suffer nerve damage. Her action delayed the drug's approval long enough for Americans to find out how harmful it really was.

After the FDA stopped thalidomide from being sold in the United States, critics at first accused it of incompetence; however, Kelsey was eventually hailed as a heroine. After Americans realized that federal regulators had prevented a drug disaster, many of them urged lawmakers to support a bill sponsored by Senator Estes Kefauver, who for years had called for closer regulation of the pharmaceutical industry.

In 1962, the Kefauver-Harris Amendments to the Food, Drug and Cosmetic Act* passed without a single "no" vote. A key provision of the law put the burden on the manufacturer to prove that a proposed new drug was effective as well as safe, and required that the proof consist of scientific studies. Ironically, the impetus for the effectiveness requirement was a drug that was effective but not safe.

Other provisions of the law required drug companies to disclose the risks of new drugs that they advertised in medical journals, and to obtain "informed consent" from those who participated in clinical drug trials. Informed consent requires those who conduct a trial to disclose all risks associated with it.

*P.L. 87-781, 79 Stat. 226–235.

medication. As Jacky Law observed: "So long as drugs have been shown to be safe and to do what is claimed of them, they are made available to doctors, the de facto brakes in the system; because why would they prescribe something if it wasn't strictly necessary?"[15]

Much of the information that doctors receive about new drugs comes from drug companies themselves. Consider the example of continuing medical education: In most states, doctors must take courses in order to keep their medical licenses current. Drug companies often provide these courses, spending more than $1 billion per year on course materials and instructors. Dr. Richard Horton, the editor of British medical journal the *Lancet*, explains how continuing medical education is used to promote drugs:

> A pharmaceutical company will sponsor a scientific meeting. Speakers will be invited to talk about a product, and they will be paid a hefty fee (several thousand pounds) for doing so. They are chosen for their known views about a particular drug or because they have a reputation for being adaptable in attitude towards the needs of the company paying their fee.
>
> The meeting takes place and the speaker delivers a talk. A pharmaceutical communications company will record this lecture and convert it into an article for publication, usually as part of a collection of papers emanating from the symposium. This collection will be offered to a medical publisher for an amount that can run into hundreds of thousands of pounds.
>
> The publisher will then seek a reputable journal to publish the papers based on the symposium, commonly as a supplement to the main journal.[16]

## Drug companies misuse clinical trials.

The FDA requires clinical trials as proof that a proposed new drug is safe and effective. Some people believe, however, that trials have become part of the drug companies' efforts to market new drugs.

Because billions of dollars in possible revenue are dependent upon FDA approval, drug companies try to maximize the chances that trials produce a favorable result. Dr. Marcia Angell observes, "Trials are rigged in a dozen ways and it happens all the time."[17] She describes some techniques that companies use: conducting trials in multiple countries to give the impression of a larger number of successes; giving new drugs to younger, healthier patients instead of to people representative of the population that will actually take them; ending trials before a drug's long-term effects are known; and suppressing unfavorable results.

The results of clinical trials are reported in medical journals, but some question the way in which results are presented. Dr. Lawrence Altman, a professor of medicine at New York University, explains:

> Journals have devolved into information-laundering operations for the pharmaceutical industry. . . .
>
> The journals rely on revenues from industry advertisements. But because journals also profit handsomely by selling drug companies' reprints of articles reporting findings from large clinical trials involving their products, editors may "face a frighteningly stark conflict of interest" in deciding whether to publish such a study.[18]

In some instances, drug companies even "ghost-write" articles. For example, Dr. Jeffrey Lisse, a rheumatologist at the University of Arizona, was listed as the lead author of an article about a Vioxx study conducted by Merck & Co. Lisse, however, revealed that his participation in that study was limited:

> Merck designed the trial, paid for the trial, ran the trial. Merck came to me after the study was completed and said, "We want your help to work on the paper." The initial paper was written at Merck, and then it was sent to me for editing . . .

Basically, I went with the cardiovascular data that was presented to me.[19]

## Post-approval regulation is weak.

Post-approval, or "Phase IV," trials are the exception, not the rule, and drug companies have little incentive to conduct them unless they know in advance what the outcome will be. (See "The Clinical-Trial Process" on page 44.) As Dr. Jerry Avorn observed, "Discover a new drug and you can profit from doing so; the same is not true for the discovery of a new drug side effect."[20] However, drug companies do conduct post-approval studies in hopes of discovering "off-label" uses—that is, treating conditions other than the ones for which the drug had been approved. They then rely on their huge sales forces to visit doctors and inform them of off-label uses.

Some believe that the FDA lost its independence after Congress passed the Prescription Drug User Fee Act in 1992. Under that law, a drug company can pay a fee—currently, $576,000—to the FDA in exchange for accelerated review of a proposed new drug. A study by the U.S. Government Accounting Office suggests that the accelerated review has made it more likely that unsafe drugs will come to market. The GAO found that the recall rate for already-approved drugs rose from 1.56 percent between 1993 and 1996 to 5.35 percent between 1997 and 2001. Regulators contend that hasty approval is incompatible with protecting the public. Dr. John Griffin, who worked at the British counterpart of the FDA, observed that "[t]halidomide is an excellent example of how regulators should not allow themselves to be hustled to approve drugs for marketing reasons."[21]

## The pharmaceutical industry has too much influence over the government.

One common complaint about drug companies is that they have used their wealth to buy political influence. The pharmaceutical industry is among the biggest spenders on lobbying and the

# Checks and measures in drug making

It takes years to develop a new drug and at every stage harmful side effects are evaluated. Recent Senate testimony criticized the Food and Drug Administration, which supervises the management of drug design.

**A typical path of a new drug from research to market**

| An idea for a drug is formed | Animal testing follows | the drug over a few months |
|---|---|---|

The process begins with chemical analysis and the isolation of potential treatments

The documents are submitted to FDA

Small group of healthy human volunteers take

More than several hundred people with disease take the drug for up to two years

A larger group of people take the drug for one to four years. Data is collected and analysis done to form warning labels

Drug is approved for marketing

Manufacturer can voluntarily inform public as information arise

---

SOURCE: Food and Drug Administration's Center for Drug Evaluation and Research

AP

**The graphic above shows the different steps a drug goes through before being released to the market. All prescription drugs must be tested extensively in labs before drug companies are permitted to sell them to consumers.**

most generous contributors to candidates for office. According to the Center for Responsive Politics, drug companies together donated more than $29 million to candidates during the 2002 election cycle. Of that money, 74 percent went to Republicans who at the time controlled both houses of Congress and set the legislative agenda.[22]

Some critics believe that the pharmaceutical industry was repaid for those contributions in the form of favorable Medicare legislation. In 2003 Congress passed Medicare Part D, the

## Should Vioxx Have Been Withdrawn Sooner?

Five and a half years after the FDA approved Vioxx, Merck & Company withdrew it from the market. Merck's critics argue that it should have done so years earlier.

Vioxx, like many other drugs, was designed to solve one problem but inadvertently created a new one. Merck had tried to solve the problem created when common pain relievers damage a person's stomach or intestines. Scientists estimated that each year those side effects kill more than 16,000 of the Americans who take pain-relief products. During the 1990s, Merck's scientists discovered that the human stomach contained two different but closely related enzymes, or proteins, and that one attacked the stomach lining while the other did not. They developed Vioxx, which attacked only the harmful enzyme.

The results of a study called VIGOR, released in November 2000, suggested that patients who took Vioxx for more than a month had a significantly higher risk of heart attacks than those who took an existing pain reliever called naproxen, which is sold under the brand name Aleve. Several months later, Dr. Eric Topol, a heart specialist at the Cleveland Clinic, and two of his colleagues published their own analysis of the VIGOR data in the *Journal of the American Medical Association*. Based on their findings, they challenged the safety of Vioxx and called for more studies to settle the issue.

Merck argued that Vioxx was not to blame for the higher risk of heart attacks. The company contended that the added heart attack risk occurred among those who were at high risk already on account of a previous heart attack, and who should have taken aspirin as well as Vioxx. It also maintained that patients in the naproxen group had fewer heart attacks because naproxen protected the prescription drug benefit for older Americans. Some argue that drug companies hijacked the legislation. Said Jacky Law:

> The law has been described as a giveaway to industry on two counts. The first is because it uses the private insurance system, which is more responsive to patient demand for the latest medicines (because insurers have various ways they can pass prices on . . .). The second and more significant reason is that there is a specific clause in the law that forbids the Department

heart—a claim that later studies neither proved nor disproved. Later, Merck also pointed to other studies that indicated Vioxx was not linked to an increased risk of heart attacks.

While the merits of Vioxx were being debated, Merck drew criticism for continuing to market the drug—and, in particular, for continuing to advertise it directly to consumers. Merck finally withdrew Vioxx from the market in September 2004, shortly after the results of another study it commissioned, known as APPROVe (Adenomatous Polyp Prevention on VIOXX trial), became public. The APPROVe study indicated that Vioxx users had twice as many heart attacks and strokes as patients who took a placebo. Merck then argued—and still does—that Vioxx is no more dangerous than other drugs in the same class, such as Celebrex, which remains on the market.

The recall of Vioxx did not end the debate. In November 2004, the British journal the *Lancet* published an article that analyzed the studies of Vioxx available at that time. The authors concluded that on account of the "known cardiovascular risk," Merck should have withdrawn the drug several years earlier. The *Lancet* also published an editorial that criticized both Merck and the FDA for having taken so long to act. Still, though, in early 2005, an FDA advisory panel voted 17 to 15 to recommend that Vioxx be allowed back on the market.

Meanwhile, Merck faces more than 27,000 lawsuits by patients who suffered heart attacks or strokes after taking the drug. The company has announced that it will vigorously defend itself. Its principal argument in court is that the victim had so many other risk factors, such as obesity and high cholesterol, that it could not be proved that Vioxx was the cause of his heart attack. As of February 2007, Merck had won 9 of the 13 cases that went to trial.

of Health and Human Services from negotiating drug prices. The U.S. government must pay what pharma charges, in other words, a situation that is unique in the world.[23]

There is also a "revolving door" between the FDA and pharmaceutical industry. In January 2005, Billy Tauzin was named the new president of the Pharmaceutical Research and Manufacturers of America. Tauzin had just retired from the U.S. House of Representatives, where he chaired the powerful Energy and Commerce Committee. Jacky Law commented, "Tauzin was a fairly natural choice to represent pharma interests in these difficult times, and his appointment shows the importance of friends in pharma politics."[24]

Finally, supporters of regulation argue that consumers need the FDA because the pharmaceutical industry cannot police itself. Philip Hilts related the story of a business school professor who had his students play the role of the board of directors of a drug company. The student "directors" voted to keep a drug on the market even after they learned of its deadly side effects. That result does not surprise Hilts, who observed:

> This is the reason for regulation. We must recognize the roles business managers are required to play, and simply set in counterposition to them a group with a fundamentally different role. Against businesses, whose first job is profit, we must set groups whose first job is safety. It is, after all, common sense.[25]

### Americans have become "over-medicated."

In 2004, more than 3.1 billion prescriptions were written in the United States. One reason for the wide acceptance of prescription drug use is that drug companies promote them heavily, and do so directly to patients through print, television, and Internet advertising.

These days, many Americans take more than one prescription drug, which has created a new problem called "polypharmacy." Dr. Marcia Angell explains: "When several drugs are taken at once, those other effects may add up. There may also be drug interactions, in which one drug blocks the action of another or delays its metabolism so that its action and side effects are increased."[26]

Polypharmacy, in turn, can lead to an even worse problem called the "cascade." Dr. Lori Daiello, who studies the effects of drugs on older patients, explains:

> A medication—drug number 1—causes an adverse effect that is interpreted as a new medical condition. Drug number 2 is then prescribed to treat this "new" condition. Drug number 2 causes an adverse drug effect or interaction, interpreted as a new condition, so drug number 3 is prescribed, and so on.[27]

In 2002, 28 percent of all hospital admissions of older Americans were due to medication problems, at a cost of $20 billion per year.

## Summary

The pharmaceutical industry is immensely profitable, but critics maintain that it puts profits above public health. Drug companies spend heavily on influencing the political process and, in doing so, have weakened the government's system of drug regulation. Companies' emphasis on "blockbuster" drugs has resulted in medications that are no more effective than those already on the market and, in some cases, dangerous drugs that were rushed through the approval process. Aggressive efforts to market drugs have changed the medical practice for the worse by encouraging doctors to prescribe medication rather than treat the conditions patients complain of.

# Regulation Is More Dangerous Than Drug Side Effects

O n several occasions, drug disasters have led to closer regulation of the pharmaceutical industry. Elixir Sulfanilamide was followed by passage of the Food, Drug and Cosmetic Act, and thalidomide by the effectiveness requirement for new drugs. It appears that Vioxx has led the FDA to take an increasingly cautious approach to new drugs. Andrew Pollack, a reporter for the *New York Times*, observed:

> Even if there have been no official policy changes, though, people close to the FDA say the agency's drug reviewers have become worried they will be hauled before Congress if they approve a drug that is later found to be unsafe. The lack of a permanent FDA commissioner for the last year, along with severe budgetary constraints, are also cited as factors behind delays and rejections of drug applications.[28]

Some observers believe that Congress and the FDA have once again overreacted.

## No medication is risk-free.

Evaluating drugs is not an exact science, and it is unfair to expect new drugs to be 100 percent safe and effective. Not even over-the-counter drugs are risk-free. The *Journal of the American Medical Association* reported that between 2004 and 2005, more than 700,000 Americans suffered reactions to over-the-counter drugs, and that 1 in 7 reactions resulted in hospitalization. Common pain medications have been linked to so many instances of side effects, including liver failure, that the FDA recently began the process of adopting a rule requiring manufacturers to provide stronger warnings to consumers.

Even though a drug may cause side effects, its benefits may greatly outweigh its risks. Dr. Jerry Avorn cites the example of vaccines: "Vaccinate 100,000 kids against measles, for example, and a few will develop complications, sometimes severe ones. This is tragic when it occurs, but children as a whole are far better off because measles vaccine is available."[29] Avorn adds that it is impossible to identify all possible side effects that a new drug might cause:

> It just isn't possible to conduct a new randomized controlled clinical trial for every question we need answered about a drug's effectiveness or side effects. Each new hypothesis would require many additional years of study, and tens of millions of dollars per trial, even if it were practical.[30]

Risks cannot be eliminated; rather, they can only be reduced to an acceptable level.

## Clinical trials cannot uncover all risks.

Even though clinical trials are the "gold standard" of drug evaluation, no number of trials will uncover every possible side effect or interaction with other substances. Human beings differ in age, health, and genetic makeup, and many take multiple drugs at the same time. Dr. Steven Galson, the director of the FDA's Center for Drug Evaluation and Research, explained:

> We know that when a drug is approved, because of the way clinical trials are designed, we're never going to know

## Ban On Drug Price Advertising Overturned

In the mid sixteenth century, England's Royal College of Physicians enforced a monopoly on information about drugs, including keeping the names of medicines a secret from the public. That attitude persisted into modern times, with doctors and pharmacists believing that patients were not capable of evaluating prescription drugs. They supported laws that restricted the flow of information, even to the point of barring pharmacies from advertising the price of the drugs they sold.

During the 1970s, consumer groups argued that restrictions on price advertising were unfair. They found that drug prices varied widely and, as a result, consumers—especially the poor and those on fixed incomes—had no idea whether they were being overcharged. One consumer group, the Virginia Citizens Consumer Council, challenged a state law under which a pharmacist who advertised drug prices was guilty of "unprofessional conduct," an offense that could result in the loss of his or her license. The council raised a novel argument—namely, that the law violated the First Amendment's guarantee of freedom of speech because it deprived the *audience* of speech. The council's challenge ultimately came before the U.S. Supreme Court which, in *Virginia State Board of Pharmacy v. Virginia Citizens Consumer Council* (1976), ruled that the advertising ban was unconstitutional. The vote was 8 to 1.

Justice Harry Blackmun wrote the majority opinion for the Court. Following the reasoning of recent Court decisions at that time, he concluded that the First Amendment protected "commercial speech," so long as it was truthful and did not pertain to illegal transactions. Even though Virginia argued that the advertising ban was necessary to maintain professionalism, Justice Blackmun found that the state could not further that interest "by keeping the public in ignorance of everything about how a drug works and whether it causes adverse events. We just can't study the drugs in enough people to know that. . . . Right now we know when a drug is approved that we're not going to know everything.[31]

Galson added that some adverse events, like the heart problems suffered by those who took Vioxx, do not come to light until

the entirely lawful terms that competing pharmacists are offering." He added that other laws helped promote professionalism among the state's pharmacists.

Justice Blackmun also found that advertising was important to the functioning of a market economy. He wrote: "So long as we preserve a predominantly free enterprise economy, the allocation of our resources in large measure will be made through numerous private economic decisions. It is a matter of public interest that those decisions, in the aggregate, be intelligent and well informed."

Justice William Rehnquist dissented. He first questioned whether the Virginia law directly affected the consumer council's interests, since it applied only to pharmacists. He pointed out that a consumer could not only ask a pharmacist how much a drug costs, but could also republish that information without violating the law. Justice Rehnquist also maintained that states had the power to regulate advertising—even truthful advertising of legal products and services—that might be detrimental to the public welfare. He wrote:

> Under the Court's opinion the way will be open not only for dissemination of price information but for active promotion of prescription drugs, liquor, cigarettes, and other products the use of which it has previously been thought desirable to discourage.

He also warned that unrestricted advertising might encourage patients to pressure their doctors to prescribe the drugs advertised to them, or even use them illegally. In addition, he insisted that society had an interest in not encouraging "drug use for every ill, real or imaginary." Critics of today's drug advertising believe that Justice Rehnquist's worst fears have come true.

**Source:** *Virginia State Board of Pharmacy v. Virginia Citizens Consumer Council*, 425 U.S. 748 (1976).

many years after a drug has been approved. Liver disease is one such effect. Neil Kaplowitz, a professor at the University of Southern California and the author of a textbook on liver disease, wrote that it would require 30,000 study patients to identify acute liver failure to the satisfaction of the scientific community. However, most drugs are approved after being given to 3,000 patients—an extensive undertaking in itself.

Finally, even large and expensive trials can yield inconclusive results. As Clifton Leaf pointed out in *Fortune* magazine:

> Enormous trials have offered conflicting data to justify or reject mammograms in younger women and PSA tests for prostate cancer; battles rage over whether synthesized GDNF (a nerve growth factor) works in Parkinson's disease and how low cholesterol levels should be in healthy people. Does flu vaccine make sense for children under 2? After 51 studies involving 263,987 children around the world, we still don't know.[32]

## The FDA over-emphasizes the risks of new drugs.

Richard Epstein, a law professor at the University of Chicago, argues that regulators can make two different types of errors when deciding whether to approve a new drug:

> Type I error arises when a drug that should be kept off the market is allowed onto the market, where it causes visible harm to its users. Type II error arises when a valuable drug is kept off the market, thereby making it impossible for sick individuals to benefit from its use. As a matter of social welfare, the right decision should be to balance both types of errors, so as to minimize the total number of lives lost or seriously damaged.[33]

He argues that the FDA focuses too much on Type I error, and that focus has led it to demand increasingly expensive clinical trials. Regulatory delay costs drug manufacturers in yet another way: It shortens the term of patent protection for those drugs that are approved because a company usually patents a proposed new drug when clinical trials start. A shorter term of protection means that the drug will generate less revenue.

According to the Progress and Freedom Foundation, the elapsed time from the discovery of a new drug to its approval by the FDA rose from 6.5 years in 1964 to 14.8 years today. The Tufts Center for Drug Development questions whether the approval process needs to take so much time, especially considering that the agency's "fast-track" approval programs have not resulted in an increase in dangerous drugs on the market. The center recently reported:

> [W]e have found no evidence that links the rate of drug safety withdrawals and the passage of legislation more than a dozen years ago aimed at speeding new drug approvals. . . .
>
> In fact, the average approval time for drugs withdrawn since 1980 is shown to be slightly higher than the average approval time of all drugs during that period—2.14 years compared to 2.08 years.[34]

Finally, author Philip Hilts observes that the FDA's current standards keep most unsafe drugs off the market:

> More than 97 percent of [new drugs] are safe and effective. They are approved quickly and don't often come back to haunt reviewers, doctors, or companies. The number that do need to be pulled has remained essentially stable over the past twenty-five years at between 2 and 3 percent in the United States—a number noticeably better than in other nations reviewing drugs.[35]

To impose even higher standards would deliver little in the way of added protection.

# Merck braces for Vioxx litigation firestorm

Since Merck & Co. pulled its arthritis drug Vioxx from the market a little more than one month ago, there has been a large spike in the number of federal lawsuits against the drugmaker. The company also faces numerous state and international suits.

**Federal court litigation against Merck**
With percentage of product liability suits

| 1999 | 2000 | 2001 | 2002 | 2003 | 2004 |

May 30, 1999-Sept. 29, 2004 - **807 federal suits**

Product liability cases: 51.5%

Sept. 30-Nov. 3, 2004 - **80 federal suits**

Product liability cases: 75.0%

**State breakdown of 60 federal product liability suits filed between Sept. 30 and Nov. 3, 2004**

No suits filed in Alaska or Hawaii

SOURCE: LexisNexis CourtLink                                    AP

In a recent editorial, the *Wall Street Journal* observed, "Despite the high-profile Vioxx panic, the FDA is far more likely to kill by depriving you of a drug than allowing you to take a dangerous one." Regardless, when Merck withdrew Vioxx from the market, it faced a virtual firestorm of litigation from across the country, as demonstrated in the graphic above.

## Regulation costs more lives than it saves.

In a recent editorial, the *Wall Street Journal* observed, "Despite the high-profile Vioxx panic, the FDA is far more likely to kill by depriving you of a drug than allowing you to take a dangerous one."[36] In 1985, Dr. Dale Gieringer, a professor at Stanford University, estimated that between 1950 and 1980, FDA regulation might have prevented the deaths of 8,000 Americans, but resulted in the deaths of as many as 120,000 Americans on account of delays in getting drugs approved. Ten years later, Robert Goldberg, who is now at the Manhattan Institute's Center for Medical Progress, estimated that FDA delays resulted in the deaths of at least 200,000 Americans during the past 30 years. Many of the delayed drugs were being used safely and effectively in other countries.

One case of excessive FDA caution involves antidepressants, which carry a prominent "black-box" warning about the risk of suicide in young people who take them. It is estimated that depression affects 2 million American teenagers. Denying medication could result in more suicides resulting from untreated depression than from adverse reactions. In addition, depression reduces productivity and lessens the sufferer's ability to lead a normal life. Ed Wiesmeier, the head of student health at the University of California, Los Angeles, observed:

> There are more young people who can succeed in a university environment because of the drugs who could not have twenty years ago. The drugs allow them to succeed ... and most respond reasonably well to the [antidepressants] without a lot of counseling visits.[37]

Another instance in which the FDA's excessive caution might have been deadly involves a vaccine called RotaShield. It was proven effective in preventing a diarrhea-causing virus that causes 600,000 deaths a year, nearly all of them children. In the United States, where rotavirus is rarely deadly, it is still serious enough to send 95,000 small children to the emergency room and 227,000 to the doctor's office every year. Despite RotaShield's benefits, the FDA pressured the manufacturer to take the drug off the market after it was found to increase the occurrence of a rare bowel obstruction by 1 to 2 cases per 10,000. In response to the FDA, the manufacturer not only withdrew the drug, but also stopped work on it altogether.

Six years later, two other companies launched new rotavirus vaccines that did not increase the risk of bowel obstructions.

On the surface, it appeared that the system worked as intended: a dangerous drug was withdrawn, and the industry developed safer ones. However, as *Fortune*'s Clifton Leaf observed:

## The Clinical Trial Process

The FDA's rules governing the approval of new drugs are found in Title 21, Part 314, of the Code of Federal Regulations. Title 21, §314.50, which sets out the required contents of an application, does not refer to specific phases of clinical trials. However, a three-phase series of trials has become the standard procedure for proving that the drug is safe and effective.

The FDA itself does not test new drugs. That is done by government bodies such as the National Institutes of Health, universities, private companies, and drug companies themselves. The FDA's role is to oversee clinical trials and review their results, and to determine whether the results justify allowing the drug to be sold.

The process of developing a new drug, of course, begins by focusing on a disease. Scientists determine what causes the disease—for instance, a form of virus—and then attempt to discover or invent a drug that can attack it. Once the drug is identified, there is a significant probability that it will prove toxic to humans. As a result, scientists must proceed cautiously. Philip Hilts explains:

> [T]ests are conducted on cells, then on two or more animal species. A drug's chemistry is considered—can the drug be made reliably, its components rendered stable so it does not deteriorate on the shelf? Exposing animals to a drug can show whether it interferes with the normal chemistry of organs, whether it breaks down into other chemicals, and whether those "metabolites" are hazardous. . . . Then there are the questions about how a drug affects behavior. Do the animals become agitated when taking it, or unusually sleepy? Do they go off their feed or lose weight?*

If tests on cells and animals show promise, the drug company next files an Investigational New Drug Application with the FDA, and at the same time applies to a different federal agency for a patent—the exclusive right to market the drug—because from this point on, it is hard to keep the drug a secret from competitors.

But consider the cost of not having the vaccine during those six years: An estimated 3.6 million children have been lost worldwide to a preventable disease. And if 3.6 million deaths weren't tragic enough, further study has led some researchers to believe that the 1999 vaccine may not have caused the

The next step in the process is conducting clinical trials. Dr. Marcia Angell explains how they are conducted:

Phase I entails giving the drug to a small number of usually normal volunteers to establish safe dosage levels and study its metabolism and side effects. (The exceptions are cancer and AIDS drugs, which are tested on people with the disease even in Phase I.) If the drug looks promising, it moves into Phase II, which involves as many as a few hundred patients with the relevant disease or medical condition. The drug is given at various doses, and the effects are usually compared with those in a similar group of patients not given the drug. Finally, if all goes well, Phase III clinical trials are undertaken. These evaluate the safety and effectiveness of the drug in much larger numbers of patients (hundreds to tens of thousands), and they nearly always involve a comparison group of patients.**

Most Phase III trials are "double blind," which means that neither those who conduct the trial nor the subjects who participate in it know what medication has been given to whom.

Once the trials are completed—this process can take years—the company must file a New Drug Application with the appropriate FDA advisory committee, which reviews the application and makes a non-binding recommendation to the agency. Once the drug receives FDA approval, it can be marketed. After approval, the manufacturer may promote the drug only for the uses and dosage for which it was approved.

*Philip J. Hilts, *Protecting America's Health: The FDA, Business, and One Hundred Years of Regulation*. New York: Alfred A. Knopf, 2003, p. 228.

**Marcia Angell, M.D., *The Truth About Drug Companies: How They Deceive Us and What to Do About It*. New York: Random House, 2004, p. 27–28.

rare bowel obstruction after all: The complication sometimes occurs for no known reason.[38]

Doug Bandow of the Cato Institute cited other examples of life-saving drugs that have been kept off the market as the result of FDA inaction:

> For instance, families with a member suffering from Alzheimer's disease were frustrated by the agency's refusal to authorize, despite strong evidence of its efficacy, the use of the drug THA, which is available in other nations. Delays in bringing pro-pranolol, a beta-blocker for use in treating angina and hypertension, to the U.S. market may have cost 100,000 lives. Nearly as many may have perished from the lack of availability of the anti-bacterial medicine Depra. Thousands have also died waiting for misoprostol, a drug for gastric ulcer, and streptokinase and TPA, for heart conditions. Equally costly was the delay in bringing anti-AIDS drugs, such as AZT, to the market.[39]

Some warn that FDA inaction will lead to even more serious problems in the future. The drugs held up by regulatory delay include antibiotics that could fight mutant "superbugs" that resist currently available medications. In 1992, according to the National Institutes of Health, 13,300 patients died of an infection they acquired in the hospital. In 2004, the death toll rose to 90,000. Vaccines, including those that might protect the public against a bird flu pandemic or a bio-terror attack, have also been kept off the market by regulation.

———•———•———•———

## Summary

The FDA has become averse to risk, especially after the recall of Vioxx. The agency now demands an extremely low likelihood of adverse reactions before approving a drug, and insists that companies conduct lengthy and expensive clinical trials. In addition, the FDA focuses too much on the remote possibility that a new drug can kill patients. In doing so, it ignores an even larger problem—namely, that many more patients will die because beneficial drugs are unavailable. Regulatory caution has reduced the number of drugs in development because companies have little incentive to develop life-saving vaccines and treatments for serious illnesses that affect relatively small populations.

# Drug Prices Are Unreasonably High

J oyce Elkins, a 64-year-old retiree, had to take a drug called Mustargen to treat a rare form of cancer. While she was taking the drug, the price of a two weeks' supply jumped from $77.50 to $548.01, which Elkins had to pay out of her own pocket because her health insurance did not cover the drug. According to Alex Berenson, who told Elkins's story in the *New York Times*, "The increase has stunned doctors, who say it starkly illustrates two trends in the pharmaceutical industry: the soaring price of cancer medicines and the tendency for those prices to have little relation to the cost of developing or making the drugs."[40] Many critics believe that drug companies are taking advantage of sick and elderly patients.

### Drug companies make excessive profits.

In 2002, Americans spent $164.2 billion on prescription drugs, and much of that spending found its way to the pharmaceutical industry's bottom line. That year, America's 10 largest drug companies made nearly $36 billion in profits. Pfizer, the most profitable of the 10, made $9.1 billion, thanks to "blockbuster" drugs such as the cholesterol-lowering drug Zocor, the antidepressant Zoloft, and the allergy medicine Zyrtec. The advocacy group Public Citizen observed, "[I]t was no big surprise that the drug industry recorded large annual profits in 2002—it simply was a continuation of a trend that has stretched over three decades."[41] Public Citizen found that the drug companies in the Fortune 500 made a profit of 17 cents for every dollar of revenue and a return on assets of 14.1 percent, compared to the Fortune 500 as a whole, which has on average a profit margin of 3.1 cents and a return on assets of 2.3 percent.

Drug companies have also made their top executives rich. The advocacy group Families USA reported that in 2004, Merck CEO Raymond Gilmartin received more than $37 million in compensation—which did not include his outstanding stock options. That same year, the average drug company CEO earned $13 million. Shareholders of drug companies, which include large mutual funds, have also earned generous returns on their investments.

## Drug companies take advantage of patients.

At the same time drug companies are making huge profits, the prices they charge for their products are rising. Families USA, a coalition of advocacy groups, reported, "[i]n 2004 alone, the price of the top brand-name drugs used by older Americans rose by 7.1 percent, which was more than two-and-one-half times the rate of inflation. This overall price increase is consistent with price increases seen over the past several years, and there is no reason to expect such annual increases will not continue."[42] Drugs are becoming less affordable and, as the Prescription Access Litigation Project observed, "It is not uncommon that uninsured and underinsured consumers are forced to choose between having enough to eat and purchasing their medications."[43]

Older Americans are hardest hit by rising drug costs. Legislation intended to help them pay for those drugs was introduced in Congress, but the benefit that passed, Medicare Part D, resulted in a windfall for the pharmaceutical industry. Critics believe that the Medicare drug benefit's estimated cost—$400 billion during a 10-year period—is twice as high as it should

## How Far Can States Go in Regulating Drug Prices?

A contentious issue relating to prescription drugs is whether the government should use its buying power to force drug companies to lower their prices. Critics describe that approach as a form of price control, and argue that market forces are more effective at keeping prices down. In 2003, when Congress created the Medicare drug benefit, it expressly barred the federal government from negotiating prices with drug companies.

Those who favor price negotiation argue that the government should have the same right as other buyers to ask for the best price. That approach is followed in several other federal programs. One such program is Medicaid, under which the federal government provides financial assistance to states that choose to reimburse low-income residents for the cost of medical care.

Some states offer programs that go beyond Medicaid. In 2000, Maine lawmakers created Maine Rx, a discounted-drug program for residents who lacked health insurance but did not meet Medicaid's eligibility standards. Instead of paying for lower-cost medications out of the state treasury, Maine used its buying power under Medicaid to force drug companies to lower prices for all Maine Rx beneficiaries. If a company refused to offer a drug at a discount, doctors who wished to prescribe it for a Medicaid patient would first have to obtain authorization from the state. Because the prior-authorization requirement—which the Medicaid Act allows states to impose—discourages doctors from prescribing a drug, it encourages drug companies to cut prices.

The Pharmaceutical Research and Manufacturers of America (PhRMA) filed a federal lawsuit seeking an injunction against Maine Rx—that is, a court order be because Congress barred the government from negotiating with drug companies for lower prices. By contrast, Congress permits the Department of Defense and the Department of Veterans Affairs to negotiate prices of the drugs they purchase from pharmaceutical companies. According to Public Citizen, those departments save 40 to 50 percent off the retail price of drugs.

halting the program—on the grounds that the state was using its bargaining power under Medicaid in order to benefit an entirely different program. The U.S. District Court issued an injunction, but the state appealed. The case ultimately reached the U.S. Supreme Court which, in *Pharmaceutical Research and Manufacturers of America v. Walsh*, 538 U.S. 644 (2003), ruled 6 to 3 that the injunction was improper.

Justice John Paul Stevens wrote the majority opinion. He concluded that Maine Rx furthered the goals of the Medicaid program, for example, by keeping the uninsured off the Medicaid rolls. He also found no evidence that the prior-authorization requirement interfered with the operation of Medicaid. In addition, Justice Stevens concluded that Maine Rx was not an unconstitutional interference with interstate commerce because Maine had neither attempted to regulate prices charged outside the state nor tied the price of drugs offered in Maine to those that were charged in other states.

Justice Sandra Day O'Connor dissented. She contended that Maine had used its bargaining power to fund a program unrelated to Medicaid, and therefore the district court had acted properly when it enjoined Maine Rx. She also maintained that Maine had made improper use of the prior-authorization requirement. She wrote:

> Under Maine Rx, the imposition of prior authorization is in no manner tied to the efficacy or cost-effectiveness of a particular drug. Rather, the sole trigger for prior authorization is the failure of a manufacturer or labeler to pay rebates for the benefit of non-Medicaid populations.... It is thus entirely possible that only the most efficacious and cost-effective drugs will be subject to a prior-authorization requirement under Maine Rx.

## Consumers pay drug companies' questionable expenses.

Some believe that the pharmaceutical industry inflates the cost of bringing new drugs to market. The Tufts Center for Drug Development estimated the cost of developing a new drug at $802 million, but Public Citizen insists that the figure is no more than $240 million. A report by that organization explains:

> The industry counts the opportunity cost of capital, not actual cash outlays, which inflates the estimate by about 50 percent; and the industry's analysis does not reduce the costs of R&D by 34 percent, which is the amount that is tax deductible. In addition, the study only looks at the most innovative—and therefore most expensive—drugs being developed. But about half of new drugs are "me-too" drugs, which often replicate existing successful drugs.[44]

Marketing expenses, which have risen sharply in recent years, drive up the price of drugs. The Government Accountability Office recently estimated that drug companies spent $4.2 billion on direct-to-consumer advertising, and an additional $7.2 billion promoting their products to medical professionals. Public Citizen found that drug companies' spending on advertising increased at a much greater rate (32 percent) in 2000 than did spending on research and development (13 percent). *Advertising Age* magazine reported that in 2002, Pfizer and Johnson & Johnson spent more on advertising than Coca-Cola or McDonald's.

Finally, companies' post-approval clinical trials are aimed more at discovering new ways to market a drug than confirming whether it is truly safe. Greg Critser, the author of *Generation Rx*, observes: "[T]hese trials are also commercial endeavors, now more than ever, with nonmedical aims thrumming below the surface. They are part of a sales machine, which has, in the language of clinical trials, a very different endpoint indeed."[45]

Drug companies improperly classify the costs of those trials as research-and-development expenses, which exaggerates the cost of developing new drugs.

## Drug companies engage in anti-competitive practices.

The pharmaceutical industry has been accused of stifling competition, especially with respect to patents. According to the forecasting company Global Insight, the price of a drug falls by 20 to 30 percent once the first generic drug enters the market and competes with the brand-name version. After other companies make generic versions as well—federal law gives the first company six months' exclusivity—the price falls to less than half the original price of the brand-name drug. Thus drug companies have an incentive to keep their patents in force for as long as possible. Dr. Marcia Angell explains how they do so:

> First, companies change their top-selling drugs in ways that will add three years' exclusivity, in accord with [a 1984 act of Congress]. Second, they file for multiple patents, staggered over months or even years, which serve as pretexts for lawsuits to trigger thirty-month extensions. Third, nearly every blockbuster is tested in children to get an extra six months of exclusivity, whether the drugs are likely to be used by children or not. Fourth, brand-name companies may collude with generic companies to delay their entry into the market or to keep prices high. And fifth, they may get a new patent and FDA approval for a trivial variation of their blockbuster and promote it as an "improved" version of the original.[46]

Drug companies sometimes break the law in an effort to extend their patents. The Prescription Access Litigation Project has filed more than 25 lawsuits alleging that drug companies have attempted to keep rival drugs off the market. The project cited three lawsuits that alleged anti-competitive conduct. One suit charged GlaxoSmithKline with perpetrating fraud on the U.S. Patent Office to extend patent protection for its antibiotic

## Can the FDA Regulate Tobacco? *FDA v. Brown & Williamson Tobacco Corporation*

Tobacco use is the most common cause of preventable death in the United States, accounting for more than 400,000 fatalities every year. It is also an addictive drug, and the overwhelming majority of users start using it before the age of 18, the legal age in most states.

In 1996, the FDA adopted a rule under which it moved to regulate nicotine as a drug and cigarettes as medical devices. The FDA's rule was primarily aimed at limiting young peoples' access to tobacco products. The rule imposed a series of *access regulations*, which imposed a minimum age of 18 to buy tobacco and required sellers to ask buyers younger than 27 to show photo identification, barred the distribution of free samples, and limited vending machines to adults-only locations such as bars. The rule also imposed a series of *promotion regulations*, which restricted print advertisements and billboards, outlawed the distribution of promotional items such as T-shirts or hats with a tobacco brand name, and barred tobacco companies from attaching their names to sporting events, concerts, and other such events.

The tobacco industry filed suit to block the regulations. It argued that the FDA lacked authority to regulate their product. The lawsuit reached the U.S. Supreme Court which, in *Food and Drug Administration v. Brown & Williamson Tobacco Corporation*, 529 U.S. 120 (2000), ruled 5 to 4 against the FDA.

Justice Sandra Day O'Connor wrote the majority opinion. She concluded that the FDA's rules were contrary to the language of the Food, Drug and Cosmetic Act, which required the agency to either find that a drug is safe or take it off the market. In doing so, she also rejected the FDA's argument that regulating tobacco was permissible because that approach was safer than taking tobacco off the market entirely.

Justice O'Connor next concluded that Congress had made clear that it did not intend for the FDA to regulate tobacco. She explained:

Augmentin, and another accused the same company of listing an unenforceable patent for the pain reliever Relafen and then filing a series of frivolous suits against generic drug makers. The

> Indeed, this is not a case of simple inaction by Congress.... To the contrary, Congress has enacted several statutes addressing the particular subject of tobacco and health, creating a distinct regulatory scheme for cigarettes and smokeless tobacco. In doing so, Congress has been aware of tobacco's health hazards and its pharmacological effects.

She also concluded that the FDA's effort to regulate tobacco was inconsistent with its long-standing position that it lacked authority to do so; and, in addition, that Congress had relied on the agency's position when it passed a series of laws regulating tobacco, beginning with the Federal Cigarette Labeling and Advertising Act of 1965.

Justice John Paul Stevens dissented. He first noted that in 1938, when the Food, Drug and Cosmetic Act was passed, Congress intended to give the FDA broad regulatory authority. He also rejected the majority's conclusion that the act required the agency to take an all-or-nothing approach toward tobacco rather than the middle ground it had chosen. Justice Stevens further contended that Congress had never taken a definitive stance concerning the FDA's power to regulate tobacco. Finally, he argued that the agency was entitled to change its position in light of recent evidence of how addictive and dangerous tobacco really was.

The court's decision did not end the controversy over tobacco marketing. While this case was being appealed, the tobacco industry was facing lawsuits brought by state governments, which demanded reimbursement for the money they had paid to provide medical care for smokers. In 1998, the leading tobacco companies reached a master settlement agreement with all but a handful of states. Under that agreement, they agreed to pay more than $200 billion over a 25-year period and to take steps to discourage young people from using tobacco. Some of the restrictions on promotion and marketing to which they agreed were similar to those that the FDA had attempted to impose by rule. In addition, state officials entered into agreements with retailers to post "We Card" signs, ask for photo identification from buyers younger than 27, and take other steps to prevent underage sales.

third suit charged Bristol-Myers Squibb with illegally filing a new patent on its anti-anxiety drug Buspar, just as its original patent was to expire, to delay the entry of generic versions onto the market. The drug companies paid more than $200 million to settle the three lawsuits.

Drug companies have also been linked to other questionable practices. For example, the *Wall Street Journal*[47] recently reported on alleged anti-competitive behavior on the part of Abbott Laboratories. The drugmaker raised the price of its anti-HIV drug Norvir by 300 percent in an effort to encourage doctors to stop prescribing a "cocktail" consisting of Norvir and rival companies' drugs, and instead switch to a newer Abbott drug called Kaletra. Two AIDS patients and their labor union sued Abbott, alleging that the company violated federal antitrust laws by using a monopoly over one product to protect sales of another product.

## The public interest requires drug price regulation.

In the United States, prescription drug prices are largely unregulated. The Medicare system, the largest buyer of drugs, cannot negotiate with drug companies, and the Food and Drug Administration has no authority to regulate drug prices. The U.S. approach differs from that of other Western countries. Some governments, like those of France and Italy, directly control prices. Others do so indirectly; for example, Germany limits reimbursement under its national health-insurance plans and the United Kingdom caps drug companies' profits. Many Americans believe that it is time to adopt the European approach to drug pricing.

One argument for price regulation is that it is unethical for drug companies to profit at the expense of the sick. An example of alleged profiteering involved AZT, a treatment for the HIV virus. When Wellcome PLC's HIV drug AZT first came to market, patients were forced to pay $10,000 per year for the treatment. Advocates for AIDS patients pointed out that the initial work of developing AZT was conducted at taxpayers' expense. That is also true of other drugs. As Public Citizen reported:

> The federal government has launched some of the most medically important drugs in recent years and received little, if anything, for its investments. An internal National Institutes of Health document shows that taxpayer-funded scientists conducted 55 percent of the research projects that led to the discovery and development of the top five selling drugs in 1995.[48]

Drugs for other life-threatening conditions are expensive, too. Most new cancer drugs cost $25,000 to $50,000 per year, an amount that only the wealthy and those with adequate health insurance can afford. Some argue that drug prices are higher than necessary to recoup the costs of developing them. Alex Berenson of the *New York Times* quoted from a book written by Pfizer's chairman, Henry McKinnell: "'A number of factors go into the mix' of pricing, [McKinnell] wrote. 'Those factors consider cost of business, competition, patent status, anticipated volume, and, most important, our estimation of the income generated by sales of the product.'"[49]

A second argument for price regulation stems from the pharmaceutical industry's abuse of its market power. Angell and Arnold S. Relman observed: "Prescription drugs are not like discretionary consumer products. For millions of patients, they are necessary to health and even survival. Yet, the drug companies often behave as though their only responsibility is to their shareholders."[50] Some compare drug companies to railroads of the nineteenth century. Railroads engaged in unfair—and sometimes illegal—practices in order to maximize their profits. As a result, Congress and state legislatures passed laws that regulated them, even dictating the prices they could charge. Some argue that similar regulation is needed to curb the pharmaceutical industry's anti-competitive behavior.

## Summary

Drug companies are immensely profitable, earning billions of dollars every year. Those profits are earned at the expense of individuals who need pharmaceutical products to stay healthy. The price of many medications is too high, and drug companies are partly to blame because they overspend on advertising and engage in a variety of anti-competitive practices. Exploiting the sick for financial gain is unethical, especially because taxpayers pay much of the cost of developing drugs. The U.S. government has regulated other industries in an effort to protect the public, and now has an obligation to protect people from overreaching by drug companies.

# Drugs Are
# Fairly Priced

T he U.S. government does not control domestic drug prices, but some argue that it "influences" them. John A. Vernon, Rexford E. Santerre, and Carmelo Giaccotto of the Manhattan Institute identified four forms of influence:

1. Moral suasion, or "jawboning," which relies on publicity to shame companies into cutting prices.
2. The threat of future price controls, which leads companies to cut prices voluntarily rather than risk being forced to cut them even more in the future.
3. "Crowding out," under which government programs such as Medicare take participants away from private insurance plans.
4. Buying power, meaning that the more drugs government programs buy, the more leverage the government has in negotiating prices.[51]

These measures are politically attractive, but defenders of the pharmaceutical industry maintain that in the long run, they will force patients to pay a higher price in the form of more disease, a diminished quality of life, and shorter life expectancy.

## Prescription drugs have improved the quality of life.

Dr. Jerry Avorn maintains that the U.S. pharmaceutical industry has a remarkable record of innovation. It has produced anti-psychotic medications, which keep people out of mental hospitals and enable them to live independently; beta-blockers, which lower the risk that someone who has suffered a heart attack will have another one; and antibiotics, which dramatically reduce the number of deaths caused by infections. Because drugs are constantly improving, Avorn believes that it is unfair to compare them to that of other commodities. He wrote:

> A loaf of bread or a single-family house bought in 2004 may well be no better than the same commodity bought in 1974 (and in the case of the bread, it may even be worse). But today's medications are much better products than the drugs of thirty years ago, a fact often neglected in these calculations. It's therefore helpful to consider a different comparison.[52]

In fact, prescription drugs are a bargain, because their benefits exceed their cost. According to a position paper on the Web site of the Pharmaceutical Research and Manufacturers of America (PhRMA):

> [A] study by Columbia University economist Frank Lichtenberg found that while treating conditions with newer medicines instead of older ones increases medicine costs, it significantly lowers non-drug medical spending. The study found that each additional dollar spent on using a newer prescription medicine (instead of an older one) saves roughly $7.20 in other health care costs.[53]

PhRMA noted that prescription drugs resulted in a 19 percent decrease in overall spending to treat depression and a 30 percent overall decrease in the cost of treating Alzheimer's disease patients, as well as a 70 percent decline in the death rate from AIDS, a several-percent increase in the cancer survival rate, and the potential to prevent 40,000 strokes a year. According to a study by the National Bureau of Economic Research, new medications were responsible for 40 percent of the increase in life expectancy in America between 1980 and 2000, which translates into 0.8 extra years for men and 1.6 extra years for women.[54]

## Drug companies should be rewarded for innovation.

It is a basic principle of capitalism that the greater the risk, the greater the potential reward. The risks involved in developing new drugs are formidable. Because the FDA follows a strict standard as to whether a drug is "safe and effective," only 1 out of 5,000 new drugs makes it through the approval process. Worse yet, only 30 percent of those drugs that are approved ever earn a profit. Because it costs hundreds of millions of dollars to get a new drug to market, companies have no choice but to rely on revenue from "blockbuster" drugs to cover losses from drugs that never even win FDA approval.

Drug "dry holes" are expensive. In December 2006, Pfizer announced that it had halted clinical trials on torceptrapib, a drug intended to increase "good" cholesterol levels, after trial participants who took the drug had a higher death rate than those who did not. In an editorial, the *Wall Street Journal* observed, "In the case of torceptrapib, Pfizer's loss in sunk R&D [research and development] costs was something approaching $1 billion, which is not atypical in developing any new drug. That's not to mention 15 years of effort."[55] However, companies have no choice but to keep making risky investments in order to develop replacements for those drugs whose patent protection will expire.

## Drug companies are unfairly accused of greed.

Even though oil, auto, and computer companies have all earned huge profits at one time or another, the pharmaceutical industry has been singled out for criticism. Defenders call the harshest criticism unfair. First of all, the pharmaceutical industry is

# Michigan's "Drug Shield" Law

In 1995, the Michigan legislature became the first and only state to pass a "drug shield" law. It is codified as §600.2946, subsection (5), of the Michigan Compiled Laws Annotated. The law provides:

In a product liability action against a manufacturer or seller, a product that is a drug is not defective or unreasonably dangerous, and the manufacturer or seller is not liable, if the drug was approved for safety and efficacy by the United States food and drug administration, and the drug and its labeling were in compliance with the United States food and drug administration's approval at the time the drug left the control of the manufacturer or seller. However, this subsection does not apply to a drug that is sold in the United States after the effective date of an order of the United States food and drug administration to remove the drug from the market or to withdraw its approval. This subsection does not apply if the defendant at any time before the event that allegedly caused the injury does any of the following:

(a) Intentionally withholds from or misrepresents to the United States food and drug administration information concerning the drug that is required to be submitted under the [Food, Drug, and Cosmetic Act], and the drug would not have been approved, or the [Food and Drug Administration] would have withdrawn approval for the drug if the information were accurately submitted.

(b) Makes an illegal payment to an official or employee of the United States food and drug administration for the purpose of securing or maintaining approval of the drug.

Governor John Engler, who signed Michigan's drug-immunity law, later said of it:

cyclical. Richard Epstein, a law professor at the University of Chicago, warns that the current "up" cycle might be ending:

> The huge profits of major drug firms are often tied to one or two drugs, such as Pfizer's Lipitor or Viagra—profits that

I believe that for something like drugs, national standards make a lot of sense. Federal regulators such as the FDA must do their job well, and we should be able to rely on them. I think the Michigan law reflects a rational approach, and a federal law modeled after it would be a rational way to protect bringing new products to market.*

Supporters of drug-shield laws also argue that the threat of lawsuits can harm public health by encouraging drug makers to withdraw products or to issue new warnings that over-emphasize risks and discourage doctors from prescribing beneficial medications. In addition, they point out that a substantial portion of the damage awards paid by drug companies go to trial lawyers, not to those injured by the drugs.

Opponents raise a number of arguments against the drug-shield law. First of all, they find it unfair because patients who are injured by the side effects of drugs—and who often incur large medical bills and suffer loss of income as well—are shut out of court. They also find the law's approach inconsistent with other areas of product liability law, where federal regulations are seen as a "floor," or minimum standard, and judges and juries are free to adopt stricter standards of whether a product is safe. In addition, given drug companies' influence over the FDA's approval process, drug-shield law opponents believe that there must be some outside check on the agency. Henry Greenspan, a professor at the University of Michigan, adds that the shield law protects those drug makers that hide the risks associated with their products, not those that take reasonable and timely action to disclose a product's risks and respond to danger signals.

In February 2007, the Michigan House voted to repeal the drug shield law; however, the repeal faces an uncertain future in the state senate.

*Stephanie Mencimer, *Blocking the Courthouse Door: How the Republican Party and Its Corporate Allies Are Taking Away Your Right to Sue.* New York: Free Press, 2006, p. 217.

evaporate when their patents expire and generics enter the marketplace. The Standard & Poor's review of pharmaceuticals thus starts somberly, noting that products with $21 billion in U.S. drug sales are going off patent in 2006, with another $24 billion to follow over the next three years— a sharp dent for an industry that today generates about $250 billion in revenue.[56]

In addition to expiring patents, drug companies face growing competition from generic drugs. Furthermore, the FDA's restrictive approach to approval is forcing companies to abandon more drugs during trials, resulting in huge investment losses. Meanwhile, Congress is poised to impose still more restrictions, and health insurers and state Medicaid administrators are demanding even lower drug prices. Some even believe that a new era has begun in which fewer breakthrough medicines will be developed.

Responding to accusations that they unfairly profit from "me-too" drugs, drug companies insist that those drugs are different and, more importantly, affect patients differently. Professor Richard Epstein adds that these drugs "reflect and create competition among drug and device manufacturers, and that competition is also a powerful driver of better quality and lower cost."[57]

Finally, defenders of the pharmaceutical industry insist that the "affordability crisis" is exaggerated. According to Doug Bandow of the Cato Institute, "In 2001, just over 8 percent of Medicare beneficiaries spent $2,000 or more annually on pharmaceuticals. The average senior spends more than twice as much on entertainment than on medicine."[58] Bandow also pointed out that even after accounting for inflation, drugs are cheaper today than they were in 1960.

In any event, few patients are denied the drugs they need. In April 2005, PhRMA launched the Partnership for Prescription Assistance Program (www.pprx.org), under which patients who lack prescription drug coverage can learn about private and public programs that might help them get the drugs they otherwise

As drug prices increase, many Americans have begun to look to Canadian pharmacies, which often sell the same drug formulas available in the United States at lower prices. Drug companies like Pfizer have lobbied to make such purchases illegal, which has raised the ire of groups like the Alliance for Retired Americans, whose members are shown demonstrating above.

could not afford. PhRMA also points out that pharmaceutical companies have distributed more than $16 billion worth of free samples to doctors. Those samples provide a "safety net" for low-income patients.

## Price controls are bad policy.

History has shown that price controls eventually do more harm than good. Bandow observed:

> Their experience running back to ancient times is extremely poor. They inflate demand, depress supply, create shortages, shift activity to unregulated sectors, and encourage wasteful avoidance and evasion activity. They also drift toward more complicated controls, entrench vested interests, take on a life of their own, and become extremely difficult to dismantle.[59]

It has been argued that price controls are inappropriate for drugs. The U.S. government has tended to regulate only the so-called "network industries," such as the telephone, railroad, electric, and power industries, which have monopoly power. In the pharmaceutical industry, however, a number of large drug companies compete against one another. Some also contend that controlling drug prices is even worse policy than controlling the prices of other goods and services. A panel of economists, led by Nobel Prize winner Milton Friedman, argued:

> Drug price controls are more difficult to remove than other price controls. Controls on oil and other products tend to be limited or short-lived, as voters eventually object to the result-ing shortages and distortions. The effects of drug price con-trols, however, are far more difficult to observe because they mainly affect medicines that haven't been invented yet.[60]

Opponents of price controls also question regulators' ability to deal with the age-old problem of scarcity. Dr. Jerry Avorn explains:

> If widespread use of cholesterol-lowering drugs in the elderly saves lives, this would be an easy problem if it cost only $100 per life saved. But these drugs can be costly; what if a widespread program of such prescribing ended up costing

$1,000,000 per life saved? Is any dollar amount too high to save a human life? If there is no limit, who's to pay?[61]

If society cannot afford all the drugs that patients need, there must be some method of deciding who gets them and who does not. Advocates of a free market insist that pricing is fairer than regulation. Professor emeritus Alain Enthoven and doctoral student Kyna Fong, both of Stanford University, make the following arguments:

> How can the government determine what price is "fair," what price appropriately reimburses pharmaceutical companies for all their research and development efforts? How can the government determine what prices will encourage the right levels of future innovation? The government negotiating prices only leaves room for additional gains through political lobbying and campaigning, activities at which pharmaceutical companies have proven themselves rather adept.[62]

## Price controls diminish the quality of care.

Medical progress is often measured in "life-years," added years of life resulting from advances such as new drugs. Free-market advocates maintain that price controls hurt patients in the form of lost life-years. John Vernon, Rexford Santerre, and Carmelo Giaccotto of the Manhattan Institute estimate that between 1960 and 2001, federal influence on drug prices cost Americans 140 million life-years. Price controls are costly as well. A 2003 survey showed that Americans valued a single life-year at $160,000.

Even though the drugs that Americans buy in other countries are cheaper, advocacy groups maintain that those savings are offset by increased risks. Richard Epstein explains:

> First, once it is known that these drugs are destined for export, foreign governments will probably not incur the costs of inspection for drugs not consumed by their own citizens.

Instead, they will develop some system to segregate the products for domestic use from those for export, which seems to be the position in Canada today. Second, even if foreign governments did not follow this strategy, nothing that is done in any designated company blocks the risk of contamination or

# Do FDA Rules Bar Lawsuits Against Drug Makers?

For a number of years, the pharmaceutical industry and its supporters have complained that lawsuits allow judges and juries to second-guess the FDA's expert determination that a drug is safe and effective. They further contend that because lawsuits are brought under state law, not federal, they create a patchwork of legal standards across the country.

Drug companies and the FDA have recently raised a new defense to lawsuits—namely, that they are barred by the doctrine of *federal pre-emption*. Article VI, Paragraph 2 of the U.S. Constitution provides:

> This Constitution, and the Laws of the United States which shall be made in Pursuance thereof; and all Treaties made, or which shall be made, under the authority of the United States, shall be the supreme Law of the land.

Under the so-called Supremacy Clause, state laws that conflict with federal laws have no effect. In the case of prescription drugs, the federal law involved is the Food, Drug and Cosmetic Act and the FDA's rules implementing it, and the state law involved is that which governs liability for unsafe products.

The issue of pre-emption came to a head in 2006, when the FDA adopted a new rule* that regulated the labeling of prescription drugs. The preamble to that rule stated that labeling standards would pre-empt most lawsuits in which a drug company is accused of failing to warn patients that its product was dangerous.

One early test of that rule arose in Pennsylvania. It began when two-year-old Andreas Perry developed cancer after he was prescribed Elidol, a drug used to treat a painful skin condition called eczema. Andreas's parents sued Novartis in the U.S. District Court for the Eastern District of Pennsylvania. They alleged that the company failed to adequately warn them that Elidel might cause cancer.

adulteration thereafter. The longer the chain of custody, the greater the health risks—period.[63]

Epstein and others also maintain that the importation of drugs also means importation of other countries' price controls, and

---

Novartis moved to dismiss the lawsuit. The company—and the FDA, which intervened in the case—argued that the lawsuit was barred because, at the time Elidel was prescribed for Andreas, the FDA had not required Novartis to add a cancer warning to its packaging.

In *Perry v. Novartis Pharmaceutical Corporation*, No. 05-5350 (U.S. Dist. Ct., E.D. Pa., October 16, 2006), the district court denied Novartis's motion. It concluded that a preamble to an FDA rule was not a statement of the law but merely an advisory opinion; and that even if the preamble had legal effect, it could not be applied retroactively to 2003, when the drug was prescribed to Andreas. The district court also found that the FDA did not explicitly reject stronger warnings for Elidil, but instead simply failed to decide whether they were needed. By contrast, the same court dismissed a different failure-to-warn lawsuit, *Colacicco v. Apotex, Inc.*, 432 F. Supp. 2d 514 (E.D. Pa. 2006), because, in that case, the FDA had "specifically and repeatedly" rejected calls for stronger warnings that certain antidepressants increased the risk of suicide attempts.

The district court also concluded that the Perry family's lawsuit did not conflict with the Food, Drug and Cosmetic Act. The court pointed out that the FDA's labeling rules did not bar a drug manufacturer from warning of side effects by other means, such as sending an advisory to doctors. The district court went on to conclude:

> Requiring Novartis to add a warning to the Elidel label would not disturb the balance of the regulatory scheme since FDA regulations make specific accommodation for adding a warning in the situation the Perrys allege. Indeed, given the recent concerns about the effectiveness of the FDA's safety monitoring of recently approved drugs ... the availability of state law tort suits provides an important backstop to the federal regulatory scheme.

*71 *Federal Register* 3922, January 24, 2006.

the diminished quality of health care that accompanies them. According to PhRMA, government health regulators often decline to authorize new—and more effective—medications because of their cost. For example, relatively few patients in Germany and Italy are given cholesterol-lowering drugs to fight heart disease; in Australia, patients do not receive an important medication that prevents osteoporosis until after he or she breaks a bone, when it may be too late. Thus citizens receive a lower quality of care because of the government's efforts to hold down drug costs.

## Summary

A free market makes it possible for drug companies to develop the "wonder drugs" that eliminate some diseases and successfully treat many others. In recent years, however, government regulators have interfered with market forces by pressuring companies to lower the price of drugs. Price controls are politically popular, but they do more harm than good by depriving drug companies of the revenue they need to develop new medications. Price controls also make it impossible for companies to recoup what they spend on potential new drugs, only a few of which ever win FDA approval. Most Americans can afford the medications they need, and the pharmaceutical industry sponsors programs to help those who cannot.

# Drugs Should Not Be Marketed Like Other Products

Thomas Moore, a health policy analyst at George Washington University, explained to a congressional panel the importance of scientific analysis. He told lawmakers that a supermarket near his home sold a deadly rat poison, and that the drugstore next door sold the same substance as a drug to prevent fatal strokes. A series of "expensive, lengthy, well-designed clinical tests," Moore added, "had demonstrated that for a specific medical use, this rat poison had benefits that greatly outweighed its risks."[64] Some critics, such as Philip Hilts, fear that the science that has protected us from unsafe drugs is now in jeopardy. He observed that "[t]here is social and cultural damage done as well by the attitude of the laissez-faire [free-market] doctors, columnists, and companies. It breeds contempt for the underlying science."[65]

The marketing of prescription drugs has become a contentious issue in the United States. Until the early 1980s, pharmaceutical companies advertised them to doctors, not the general public. Under pressure from the Supreme Court and consumer groups, however, the FDA allowed direct-to-consumer (DTC) advertising on a limited basis. In 1997, the agency loosened its DTC advertising rules. As a result, some drugs have been heavily advertised on television and in other media.

## Drugs are unlike other consumer products.

Moore's story is a reminder that drugs are different from other consumer products and therefore should not be marketed in the same way. As author and journalist Greg Critser observed:

> [I]n the case of pharmaceuticals, we are talking about something fundamentally different. These are potent, sophisticated chemical compounds, developed at the cost of hundreds of millions of dollars, vetted by leading scientists for safety, and then very carefully indicated for use only with the supervision of a physician. *These products actually change our body.*[66]

For that reason, drugs are marketed under stronger regulations than other consumer products.

Despite the fact that drugs are more dangerous than other products, they are promoted in much the same way. In recent years, the pharmaceutical industry has recruited marketing-oriented executives from non-drug companies. Critser observed:

> The guru of Pfizer's DTC efforts hailed from Kraft's cereal and yogurt division, and the new head of the company's Lipitor DTC program came via the Flintstones vitamin division of Bayer and the Softsoap division of Colgate. At Merck, the DTC guru came via Maxwell House coffee.[67]

Today, there is an aggressive marketing culture within the industry. One consequence of that culture is a "blockbuster" mentality, similar to that in the motion pictures. A new drug's success depends heavily on how effectively it is marketed, especially when it first goes on the market.

According to Philip Hilts, America learned the hard way that market forces alone do not guarantee the quality of drugs:

> The regulations and the government shepherding of the drug business did what the free market failed for at least sixty years to do—it weeded out the brutal, the stupid, and the needless that prevented the pharmaceutical industry from becoming a great engine of discovery and sales.[68]

He added that a government-imposed scientific standard created what amounts to a "federal seal of approval" for drugs.

## Drug advertisements discourage good medical practice.

Direct-to-consumer drug advertising has the potential to strain the doctor-patient relationship by encouraging patients to demand a heavily advertised drug, even when it is not appropriate for his or her medical condition or when generic drugs would be just as effective. Others contend that such advertising encourages healthy people to think that they need medical attention. Their doctor visits unnecessarily burden the health-care system.

Opponents of drug advertising argue that it undercuts the doctor's traditional role of protecting patients from inappropriate prescription drugs. Dr. Marcia Angell considers it essential that someone independent of the pharmaceutical industry look out for patients' interests:

> Which of us would pretend that the free market can decide whether drugs and medical devices are safe and effective? Do you really want your doctor to rely on the word of drug companies that the antibiotic prescribed for your pneumonia will work? Doctors are not wizards, and they have no way to

know whether drugs will work well unless they can rely on an impartial agency like the FDA to review the scientific data.[69]

Few consumers can make an intelligent decision about which drugs to use and how to use them. Advertising does little to encourage good decisions because it emphasizes a drug's benefits, forcing the consumer to guess as to whether a competing product—or no medication at all—would be more appropriate. Dr. Jerry Avorn noted that Norvasc became the number-one

## The Medical Profession Tackles Conflicts of Interest

In January 2006, an article in the *Journal of the American Medical Association\** proposed strict new standards aimed at limiting drug companies' influence over the medical practice. The authors asserted that "[t]he standing of the profession, as much as the integrity of the pharmaceutical and medical device industries, is jeopardized by allowing obvious conflicts to continue."

The proposals are aimed at academic medical centers because those institutions provide leadership within the medical profession, train new doctors, and are in a position to act quickly to implement the recommendations. The authors hope that their reforms will spread throughout the profession.

Specific recommendations include the following:

(1) Doctors may not accept gifts of any value from drug company representatives. Current policy allows doctors to accept small gifts.
(2) Doctors may not accept payment from drug companies for attending meetings or participating in continuing medical education programs.
(3) The practice of companies giving free samples of drugs should be eliminated, and replaced with a system in which low-income patients receive vouchers that they can use to buy their medication. The authors explained that "[t]he availability of free samples is a powerful inducement for physicians and patients to rely on medications that are expensive but not more effective. Samples also provide company representatives with access to physicians. The increasing reliance on direct-to-consumer advertising by

selling blood pressure drug in spite of what he called "very thin clinical credentials," and that millions of women continue to take estrogen-replacement drugs even though clinical trials have linked them to a number of serious side effects.

Opponents of advertising also contend that it downplays a drug's risks and increases the potential for misuse—especially by older Americans, who are less likely to read fine-print warnings about side effects. Critics believe that the problem has grown worse because the new FDA rules allow a drug company to

drug companies only heightens the tension between current marketing practices and good patient care."

(4) Doctors who have a financial relationship with the pharmaceutical industry may not sit on a committee that is responsible for buying drugs for a hospital or a medical group.

(5) Drug companies may not provide financial support to continuing medical education programs or pay doctors to attend events that they sponsor. However, companies may contribute to a medical school or teaching hospital that, in turn, supports educational programs.

(6) Doctors who teach at medical schools and hospitals may not join drug companies' speakers bureaus or publish articles that were "ghost-written" by drug companies. By following this recommendation, the authors explained, "academic leaders will be upholding the principle that faculty opinion should be data driven and not for hire."

(7) Doctors may not accept "no strings attached" contracts or grants from drug companies. A medical school or a hospital may perform research under a bona fide contract or grant with a drug company, so long as no specific researcher is identified and the institution publicly discloses the arrangement.

(8) Medical schools must enforce and monitor compliance with these guidelines.

*Troyen A. Brennan, et al., "Health Industry Practices That Create Conflicts of Interest: A Policy Proposal for Academic Medical Centers," *Journal of the American Medical Association* 295, no. 4 (January 25, 2006): 429–432.

disclose side effects in less-conspicuous places such as on its Web site or in magazines with small audiences.

Some, such as Dr. Angell, question the need to advertise drugs in the first place. She asked, "If prescription drugs are so good, why do they need to be pushed so hard? Wouldn't the world beat a path to the door of a company that produced, say, a cure for cancer? The answer is that truly good drugs don't have to be promoted very much."[70]

## Drug advertising is inappropriate and wasteful.

In his dissenting opinion in *Virginia State Board of Pharmacy v. Virginia Citizens Consumer Council, Inc.* (1976), U.S. Supreme Court Justice William Rehnquist expressed his concern over advertising drugs in the same way as other products. He wrote:

> The very real dangers that general advertising for such drugs might create in terms of encouraging, even though not sanctioning, illicit use of them by individuals for whom they have not been prescribed, or by generating patient pressure upon physicians to prescribe them, are simply not dealt with in the Court's opinion. If prescription drugs may be advertised, they may be advertised on television during family viewing time.[71]

Irv Lerner, the former head of Roche Pharmaceuticals, commented that direct-to-consumer advertising "hurts the image of the industry by lining pharma up with beer and tobacco and cosmetics."[72] In fact, some direct-to-consumer advertising has been called inappropriate. An advertisement for Paxil, an antidepressant, appeared in the Sunday *New York Times Magazine* shortly after the September 11 terrorist attacks in the United States in 2001. The ad read in part, "Millions suffer from chronic anxiety. Millions can be helped by Paxil." Critics accused Glaxo-SmithKline, the maker of Paxil, of exploiting Americans who suffered from emotional problems after the attacks.

Some observers believe that the rush to promote new drugs has led to ethical lapses. Merck was sharply criticized for continuing to promote Vioxx—and continuing to advertise it directly to consumers—even after a study indicated that it might increase a patient's risk of a heart attack. At Pfizer, an executive gave a "pep talk" to salespeople in which he reportedly said about Neurontin, a controversial anti-epilepsy drug, "I don't want to hear that safety crap either—every one of you should take one just to see there is nothing. It's a great drug."[73] The FDA also warned Pfizer about its aggressive marketing of another drug, the antidepressant Zoloft.

The economics of the prescription drug market has lead to excessive promotion. Companies derive most of their revenue from brand-name drugs that they have an exclusive right to sell because they are patented. Once the patent expires, generic drugs come on the market and the price falls dramatically. At this point, it makes little sense for the manufacturer to keep promoting the drug, even if it is highly effective.

Critics also point out that the most-promoted drugs are not necessarily the best, as indicated by the Antihypertensive and Lipid Lowering Treatment to Prevent Heart Attack Trial (ALLHAT). This study was an independent, FDA-sponsored evaluation of a new generation of brand-name drugs for high blood pressure. The ALLHAT researchers found that the new drugs were ineffective, and in some instances unsafe. Nevertheless, those drugs were heavily promoted and widely prescribed. By one estimate, more than $3 billion has been spent on them.

Finally, Dr. Jerry Avorn insists that direct-to-consumer advertising, as we know it, is wasteful:

> If we really want to increase the public's awareness of depression or incontinence or heart disease prevention, we could do so directly; those same talented people at the advertising agencies would be quite willing to put together promotions

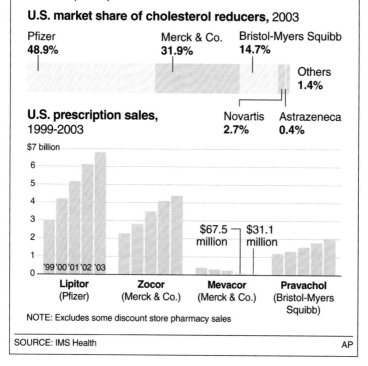

# Big business in cholesterol drugs

Two cholesterol-reducing drugs – Lipitor and Zocor – dominated pharmaceutical sales last year. Drugmakers are hoping to sell two other drugs – Mevacor and Pravachol – in the United States without a prescription.

**U.S. market share of cholesterol reducers,** 2003

Pfizer **48.9%**     Merck & Co. **31.9%**     Bristol-Myers Squibb **14.7%**

Others **1.4%**

**U.S. prescription sales,** 1999-2003     Novartis **2.7%**     Astrazeneca **0.4%**

$7 billion

**Lipitor** (Pfizer)     **Zocor** (Merck & Co.)     **Mevacor** (Merck & Co.)     **Pravachol** (Bristol-Myers Squibb)

'99 '00 '01 '02 '03

$67.5 million     $31.1 million

NOTE: Excludes some discount store pharmacy sales

SOURCE: IMS Health            AP

**Drugs like Lipitor and Zocor, which are prescribed to help lower cholesterol, have become big business for pharmaceutical companies. These companies have begun to treat such drugs like consumer products, with large budgets for advertising—a practice that many people call wasteful.**

that are not product-specific if someone paid them to do so. . . . Some might object that this is implausible—that pharmaceutical companies are willing to spend money to advertise their own products, but the nation itself lacks the resources to pay for public-interest medical messages. This is not true. In the end, the advertising bill is already being paid by the public.[74]

## An unregulated market endangers consumers.

A century ago, the Pure Food and Drug Act ended the unre-stricted marketing of medicine. Before the act took effect, "much of the medicine that was sold was worthless; the few vital ingre-dients that could be effective were often diluted with other sub-stances, faked, or mixed with dangerous ingredients. There were no national rules about hygiene, purity, or honesty in labeling foods and drugs."[75]

A 1938 amendment strengthened the original act by bar-ring unsafe drugs from the market; and 1962 legislation added the effectiveness requirement, which was enforced by the FDA through the Drug Efficiency Study Implementation program, under which government scientists identified hundreds of drugs that were either ineffective or not effective for all claimed uses. Today, ineffective prescription drugs have largely disappeared from the market.

There are, however, signs that Congress is backtracking on drug regulation. In 1994, it passed the Dietary Supplement and Health Education Act, which freed the makers of "dietary supplements" from having to prove that their products are safe and effective before marketing them. Many consider the law a mistake. For example, Philip Hilts observed, "Many of today's remedies are not just like the nineteenth-century remedies; they are the same medicines—lobelia, echinacea, pennyroyal, ephe-dra. Other, newer ones have been created in imitation of genuine scientific advances."[76]

The medical community warns that many "natural" rem-edies are risky. Dr. Jerome Groopman, a professor at Harvard Medical School, observed that "[t]he widespread misconception among the public is that what is 'natural' is necessarily salu-brious and safe, while in fact, the natural world is filled with

# Regulating "Dietary Supplements"

An estimated 60 million Americans use herbs, vitamins, and other "alternative" health-care products, and spend some $40 billion a year on them. These products are widely promoted in many ways, such as in self-help books and on the Internet. They are also largely unregulated.

In 1994, Congress passed the Dietary Supplement and Health Education Act.* It treats "dietary supplements" more like food than medicine, and subjects those products to much less regulation than prescription drugs. It sets a low standard for approval: a manufacturer can market a dietary supplement without first proving that it is safe and effective, so long as it does not advertise the product as a scientifically proven remedy for a specific health condition. If the FDA has concerns about a supplement, it has the burden of proving that the product is dangerous.

Supporters of the 1994 act argue that herbal remedies have been used by human beings for hundreds, sometimes thousands, of years and therefore do not require the same degree of regulation as the more powerful medications that are fashioned in laboratories. They also accuse the medical establishment of being biased against alternative remedies. They point out, for example, that during the early twentieth century, doctors dismissed vitamins as a fraud.

The medical and public health communities, on the other hand, believe that the act was bad legislation. Some believe that it allows companies to put "health" remedies on the market with no safety testing or FDA review, just as in the days of Elixir Sulfanilamide. They add that the law allows supplement manufacturers to make vague claims about the effectiveness of their products—for example, that it "aids the liver." Others maintain that the law exposes consumers to the risk of contaminated products, variations in potency, and the dangers of self-medication.

The recent experience with ephedra is a reminder that some dietary supplements are more powerful than people realize. Ephedra, which is derived from a shrub, has been used for thousands of years in traditional Chinese medicine to treat conditions such as asthma and hay fever. Recently, American companies found a different use for ephedra: they marketed concentrated versions of it as a weight-loss product. Because ephedra raises blood pressure and heart rate, it can cause heart attacks and strokes. An estimated 150 deaths have been blamed on the drug. One notable victim was Baltimore Orioles pitcher Steve Bechler, who used it during spring training to lose weight.

*P.L. 103-417, 108 Stat. 4331–4332.

poisons and toxins."[77] Groopman added that some "natural" remedies failed to perform as advertised. One example is Saint John's wort: "This popular herb was touted as a treatment for depression and alleged to have antiviral activity in people with HIV. It was shown to be no better than placebo for depression and, most worrisome, to interfere with the activity of the lifesaving anti-HIV protease drugs."[78] Another example is kava kava, a substance derived from the dried rhizome and roots of the kava plant. It is used to relieve stress, but it has also been linked to cases of massive liver failure. Supplement makers have been accused of failing to disclose the possible side effects of substances like kava kava, and even making false—and illegal—claims that they can cure diseases.

---

## Summary
Prescription drugs are powerful chemicals that have the potential to injure or even kill those who use them. For that reason, laws and FDA rules restrict how they may be dispensed and marketed. The recent trend toward deregulation has extended to drugs that, increasingly, are marketed in the same manner as other consumer products. In an effort to promote new products, drug companies have aired misleading advertisements and engaged in unethical marketing practices. Advertising has been blamed for disrupting the doctor-patient relationship and even encouraging unsound medical practice. Some fear that deregulation will lead to a return of the abuses of the patent-medicine era.

# A Free Market in Drugs Serves the Public

F ollowing the Pure Food and Drug Act, federal regulation of drugs has grown steadily. But some now question whether so many regulations are needed to ensure that drugs are safe and effective. The argument is that some regulations are unnecessary because information about drugs is widely available and the science of medicine has advanced considerably.

Advocates of deregulation also contend that market forces serve the public better than the government. Some go even further and insist that Americans should be able to manage their health without interference from "gatekeepers" such as doctors, pharmacists, and government officials.

### Advertising helps create better drugs.

Defenders of drug advertising argue that it benefits the public. U.S. Supreme Court Justice Harry Blackmun, who wrote the majority opinion in *Virginia State Board of Pharmacy v. Virginia Citizens*

*Consumer Council, Inc.* (1976), observed that advertising, "however tasteless and excessive it sometimes may seem, is nonetheless dissemination of information as to who is producing and selling what product, for what reason, and at what price," and added that "the free flow of commercial information is indispensable."[79]

Defenders also assert that drug advertising, like that of other products and services, stimulates competition which, in turn, results in better drugs at lower prices. For example, doctors can choose from a number of medications that treat depression or lower "bad" cholesterol levels; no one drug monopolizes the market in the treatment of a particular ailment. It has even been argued that advertising *lowers* the price of prescription drugs. That is so because a manufacturer bears most of the cost of producing a drug before it goes on the market, and advertising revenue and the increased business it stimulates helps a company recoup much of the production cost. Professor Richard Epstein explains:

> Any plausible estimate of these development costs runs into the hundreds of millions of dollars for that first pill. Without advertisement, those costs must be apportioned solely among buyers who by hook or by crook find out about the drug on their own. With information costly to acquire, that class of potential users is too small to sustain the product. That situation is known to the firm, which will not produce a drug that it cannot sell.[80]

Advertising also leads to greater sales and profits, which drug companies re-invest in the development of new drugs.

Ronald White, a professor of philosophy at the College of Mount St. Joseph, contends that the FDA's restrictions discriminate against drug advertising. He argues:

> No other industry is legally required to divulge so much unreliable, useless, and contradictory information in its advertising in order to protect the public from so many remote or

unproven harms. After all, television advertisements for sports utility vehicles are not required to divulge potential rollovers; cell phone advertisements are not required to divulge potential auto accidents; and fast-food chains are not required to divulge potential obesity from consumption of their products. [81]

## Advertising educates consumers and doctors.

A study by the Kaiser Family Foundation found that direct-to-consumer advertising has made patients more aware of treatment options and drug side effects. A 1999 survey conducted by *Prevention* magazine estimated that advertisements encouraged some 25 million people to talk for the first time with their doctors about specific health problems. Advertising also has the potential to reach millions more. According to PhRMA:

1. More than 23 million Americans who should be taking cholesterol-lowering drugs are not taking them, according to the National Institutes for Health.
2. Over 19 million Americans suffer from depression and fewer than half seek treatment.
3. Almost 6 million Americans have diabetes but don't know it or are not being treated for it.[82]

Advertising has also diminished the stigma associated with certain diseases, especially mental conditions such as depression, and has enabled people to recognize symptoms and talk to their doctor about them.

With so many drugs on the market, doctors can suffer from "information overload." Endocrinologist Richard Dolinar contends that direct-to-consumer advertising can help them. He explains:

> Let's imagine that a new drug enters the marketplace on Monday morning. . . . To make sure this new drug is available to those patients in his practice who could benefit from

## Should Dying Patients Have Access to Drugs of Their Choice? *United States v. Rutherford*

During the 1970s, cancer patients had fewer treatment options than they have today. In desperation, some patients turned to non-traditional remedies that had not been approved by the FDA. One such remedy was Laetrile, a substance derived from the seeds of fruits such as apricots.

Some states passed laws that permitted patients to use Laetrile, but the FDA refused to allow the substance to cross state lines because it had not been proven safe and effective. A number of cancer patients and their spouses filed suit challenging the agency's decision. A federal appeals court ordered the FDA to allow terminally ill patients to use the substance under a doctor's supervision. The agency appealed to the Supreme Court, which unanimously reinstated its ban on Laetrile.

Justice Thurgood Marshall wrote the court's opinion. He concluded that the "safe and effective" requirement of the Food, Drug and Cosmetic Act applied to drugs aimed at life-threatening diseases such as cancer. He found that lifting that requirement would be dangerous to those who suffered from those diseases, and warned that some patients might take untested substances instead of conventional medications that could lead to a cure. In any event, he added, the definition of "terminally ill" was unclear. Some patients who were given that diagnosis later experienced "spontaneous remission," the unexplained disappearance of symptoms.

Given the history of patent-medicine peddlers, Justice Marshall concluded that Congress reasonably could have determined that those who suffer from life-threatening diseases deserve protection from dishonest businesses. He wrote:

> Since the turn of the century, resourceful entrepreneurs have advertised a wide variety of purportedly simple and painless cures for cancer, including liniments of turpentine, mustard, oil, eggs, and ammonia; peat moss; arrangements of colored floodlamps; pastes made from glycerin and limburger cheese; mineral tablets; and "Fountain of Youth" mixtures of spices, oil, and suet.

Justice Marshall also observed that Congress had relaxed the requirements for the approval of certain anti-cancer drugs, and that an application for Laetrile's approval was presently before the FDA.

it, [the doctor] would need to sit down and review all of his charts to pick out the appropriate patients, and then notify them . . . how much more efficient it would be to have patients self-select, after seeing the DTC ad, to contact the doctor and make an appointment to see him?[83]

Dolinar added, "To be against DTC advertising is to be in favor of ignorance. Talk about a double standard."[84]

## Drug companies can regulate themselves.

In December 2006, Pfizer learned from scientists that patients who took torceptrapib, a cholesterol drug then in development, were more likely to die. Top company officials immediately halted the clinical trial and told doctors to stop prescribing the drug. An editorial in the *Wall Street Journal* praised the company's behavior and went on to observe that "Pfizer's blind trial was monitored by independent researchers, and they alerted the company that the compound appeared to increase mortality in heart patients, not decrease it as hoped."[85] The *Wall Street Journal* cited the torceptrapib incident as evidence that the pharmaceutical industry can police itself.

The industry further demonstrated that it could self-regulate by adopting voluntary guidelines for direct-to-consumer advertising.[86] The guidelines call on drug companies to show their advertisements to the FDA before airing them, discuss new drugs with doctors before starting an advertising campaign, put more emphasis on the risks of drugs, and tailor their advertising to "age-appropriate" audiences. PhRMA also created an "accountability office" to which the public can complain about offending advertisements. Likewise, dietary supplement manufacturers, which have been accused of selling worthless products and running deceptive advertising, have formed the Council for Responsible Nutrition. These efforts at self-regulation are based on "enlightened self-interest," the idea that the disreputable actions of some companies can give the entire industry a bad image and invite further regulation. Other checks on the

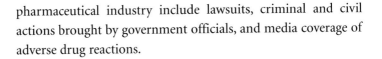
pharmaceutical industry include lawsuits, criminal and civil actions brought by government officials, and media coverage of adverse drug reactions.

## Regulators should not make decisions regarding health care.

Some believe that the FDA's decision not to approve a drug, or to order that a drug be taken off the market, intrudes on the doctor-patient relationship. According to Richard Epstein, a doctor is in the best position to judge whether a drug would in fact be dangerous for his or her patients. Epstein wrote, "[S]urely oncologists [cancer specialists] can do a better job calculating the odds than the FDA, which has to deal with averages, not individual cases."[87] Even the less-drastic step of requiring a "black box" warning for a drug interferes with medical practice. Epstein observed, "Fearful physicians thus shy away from pre-scribing such drugs—not because of the dangers the drugs pose, but because they fear the warnings expose them to greater risk of medical malpractice suits."[88]

For many of the same reasons, the FDA's limitations on "off-label" uses of drugs—uses other than that for which the agency originally approved it—have come under fire. Doug Bandow of the Cato Institute observes that "[e]xisting compounds are often found to have new uses. For example, pain relievers may help prevent Alzheimer's disease. Statins, used to lower choles-terol, appear to reduce the likelihood of strokes as well as heart attacks."[89] But the FDA's original approval for these drugs might not reflect newly acquired knowledge of their alternative uses. Worse yet, the agency's rules bar drug companies from telling the public that their products can be put to a wide range of off-label uses. Dr. Marcia Angell sums up the drug companies' complaints about the FDA: "[I]f it means that more people get prescription drugs, isn't there a net benefit? After all, the drugs are probably on balance helpful, or the FDA wouldn't have approved them and doctors wouldn't prescribe them. Shouldn't we pay more attention to the outcome and less to the process?"[90]

Regulators also have been accused of making drug-related decisions based on politics, not science. One recent example is "Plan B," a form of emergency contraception manufactured by Barr Laboratories. The FDA refused to allow over-the-counter sales of the drug until Barr agreed to make it available only to buyers who were at least 18 years old. Family-planning advocates contend that the FDA paid more attention to conservatives who feared that Plan B would encourage risky sex, especially among

## Federal Law Bars Medical Marijuana: *Gonzalez v. Raich*

How far is the reach of the federal government's power to regulate narcotics? That issue arose in a lawsuit brought by two Californian women, Angel Raich and Diane Monson. The California Compassionate Use Act entitled people with serious medical conditions to use the drug while under a doctor's care. Because of that act, Raich and Monson argued, the federal Drug Enforcement Administration had no power to stop them from obtaining marijuana.

The government defended the DEA's actions, arguing that the federal Controlled Substances Act classified marijuana as a Schedule I drug, one for which there was no legitimate use, even in the course of medical care. Because the Compassionate Use Act was in conflict with the CSA, they argued that the California act had no effect.

Under Article I, §8, of the U.S. Constitution, Congress has the power to "make all Laws which shall be necessary and proper for carrying into Execution" its authority to "regulate Commerce with foreign Nations, and among the several States." If the amount of marijuana used in medical treatment were significant enough to be considered "interstate commerce," the CSA would prevail.

The case eventually reached the U.S. Supreme Court which, in *Gonzalez v. Raich*, 545 U.S. 1 (2005), upheld the DEA's power to stop the use of medical marijuana. The vote was 6 to 3. Justice John Paul Stevens wrote the majority opinion. He first concluded that medical marijuana was not exempt from the Controlled Substances Act. The CSA, he explained, was a comprehensive law regulating narcotics, and Congress was especially concerned with the diversion of controlled drugs to illegal channels—which could happen if patients were allowed to grow and use teenagers, than to the advisory committee that voted 23 to 4 to recommend its approval.

## Regulation tramples individual liberty.

Some believe that government regulations unjustly deprive Americans of their right to choose medications that they and their doctors consider appropriate. Professor Ronald White blames "medical paternalism" for those regulations. He explains:

---

marijuana. In any event, he found no language in the CSA that exempted drugs used in the course of medical care.

Justice Stevens went on to conclude that even small quantities of marijuana used by patients like Raich and Monson had an effect on interstate commerce. He cited a 1942 Supreme Court decision, *Wickard v. Filburn*, which upheld federal limits on the growing of wheat—even when the farmer who grew it was the one using it—because overproduction defeated regulation of the interstate market in wheat. Finally, Justice Stevens suggested that the courts were not the proper forum for challenging the CSA. He wrote, "[P]erhaps even more important than these legal avenues is the democratic process, in which the voices of voters allied with these respondents may one day be heard in the halls of Congress."

There were two dissenting opinions. Justice Sandra Day O'Connor argued that the framers of the Constitution intended for the states to act as laboratories for social policy. In this case, however, the majority's interpretation of the CSA barred states from experimenting with medical marijuana, even though there was no proof that it affected interstate commerce. Justice Clarence Thomas agreed with her but went even further, arguing that the majority's definition of "commerce" was too broad. He wrote, "If the majority is to be taken seriously, the Federal Government may now regulate quilting bees, clothes drives, and potluck suppers throughout the 50 States."

The *Raich* case did not address the issue of whether marijuana belonged in Schedule I in the first place. Advocates of reforms to marijuana law have fought a long-running but unsuccessful legal battle to have the drug reclassified by the DEA. Legislation that would have created an exception in the CSA for medical marijuana died in the 109th Congress.

Medical paternalism is based on the principle that experts, usually physicians, justifiably violate their patients' liberty in order either to provide benefits or to remove harms. These benefits and harms are usually represented under the authority of objective science. The major presumption here is that health-care consumers (disguised as patients) cannot make informed pharmaceutical choices without the assistance of learned intermediaries—licensed, knowledgeable, and beneficent physicians and pharmacists who have been legally ordained as the gatekeepers of prescription drugs.[91]

Some also accuse the government of paternalism when it decides that no one may safely use certain drugs. One such drug is marijuana. A number of states allow seriously ill patients to use it under a doctor's supervision. Despite state laws, the federal government has moved to stop the use of medical marijuana because the federal Controlled Substances Act forbids doctors to prescribe the drug.

Some, like maverick psychiatrist Thomas Szasz, go even further and argue that government has no business telling people what they may put into their bodies. He wrote:

In retelling this tale, it is impossible to overemphasize that, although initially the drug laws were intended to protect people from being "abused" by drugs *others wanted to sell them*, this aim was soon replaced by that of protecting them from "abusing" drugs *they wanted to buy*. The government thus succeeded in depriving us not only of our basic right to ingest whatever we choose, but also of our right to grow, manufacture, sell, and buy agricultural products used by man since antiquity.[92]

Szasz argues that soon after Congress passed the Harrison Narcotic Act, federal officials transformed it from a consumer-protection law into a form of prohibition. They interpreted the phrase "in the course of his professional practice only" as barring a doctor from prescribing opiates to an addict to maintain the addict's habit. In *Webb v. United States* (1919), the U.S. Supreme Court agreed. It ruled that "to call such an order for the use of morphine a physician's prescription would be so plain a perversion of meaning that no discussion of the subject is required."[93] In the decades that followed, lawmakers declared more and more drugs illegal, and placed tighter controls over many others.

## Summary

The health-care professions have traditionally considered the public incapable of making intelligent decisions about drugs. This attitude of "medical paternalism" is inappropriate because people have become more knowledgeable about their own health. Some advocates believe that despite the recent trend toward deregulation, there are too many restrictions on access to drugs. They also believe that a wider variety of medications should be sold without a prescription. Defenders of direct-to-consumer advertising maintain that it educates consumers by making them aware of treatable medical conditions and more willing to visit their doctors. Free-market advocates contend that self-regulation and better-informed consumers are more effective than regulation in forcing drug companies to behave more appropriately.

# Drug Regulation in the Twenty-first Century

E very scientific advance has the potential to benefit society and, at the same time, harm it. Drugs are no exception. As Dr. Jerry Avorn observes:

> We live at the dawn of an amazing new era. Decades of brilliant progress in physiology, pharmacology, biochemistry, and now genetics have given us a capacity to prevent and treat disease that would have seemed impossible to our ancestors, or even our grandparents. Small miracles occur millions of times every day thanks to these accomplishments. But every day people also become ill or die when they don't get the drugs they need, either because their doctors didn't prescribe them or because they couldn't afford to pay for them or because they failed to take them. And the triumph of modern

pharmacology continues to be marred by lethal adverse effects that could have been averted.[94]

How to maximize the benefits and minimize the risks of these powerful substances is a matter of considerable debate.

## The Future of the FDA

During the mid 1990s, some members of Congress attempted to limit the FDA's authority. That effort failed, in part because Americans respected the agency. As Philip Hilts observes, "The simple fact is that the FDA is, at least for now, the best hope we have."[95] But lawmakers on both sides of the debate are dissatisfied with the agency, and plan to introduce legislation aimed at improving it. The Prescription Drug User Fee Act expires in 2007, and the process of renewing it is likely to spur debate over the FDA's overall role.

Whether or not lawmakers renew the user-fee system, they will almost certainly address FDA financing in general. Some, like Philip Hilts, argue that the agency is under-funded:

> In comparison with other government agencies, the FDA is tiny. It constitutes less than one half of one percent of the federal government's 2 million workers and has a budget of about $1.3 billion, less than 1/250th that of the Defense Department. Even the Agriculture Department, which focuses on a far narrower range of products and activities, is ten times larger in personnel and fifty times larger in budget.[96]

In place of user fees, some call for increased federal appropriations for the agency. Others propose charging a small fee on each of the more than 3 billion prescriptions written every year in this country.

# Expanding FDA Authority Over Already-approved Drugs

The Institute of Medicine is an organization chartered by the National Academy of Sciences. It enlists distinguished doctors and scientists to examine policy matters related to public health.

In September 2006, the institute published a report entitled *The Future of Drug Safety*.* It contained 25 recommendations, the purpose of which was to extend the FDA's pre-approval safety standards to drugs that have already been approved.

Key recommendations include the following:

(1) Expand the FDA's powers to include withdrawing approval of drugs and restricting the distribution of approved drugs—for example, by requiring specific warnings or limiting the drug to specific classes of doctors or health-care facilities.

(2) Give the FDA the power to fine companies that violate its rules.

(3) Require that newly approved drugs be identified by a distinctive symbol, such as the black triangle used for that purpose in Britain.

(4) Establish safety-related performance goals for proposed new drugs submitted under the Prescription Drug User Fee Act. The Institute of Medicine also recommended that the FDA be given enough funds to ensure that it no longer has to rely on user fees.

(5) Require drug companies to submit the results of clinical trials to the National Library of Medicine. Currently, the submission of results is voluntary.

(6) Appoint the FDA commissioner to a fixed six-year term, and provide that the president of the United States can remove the commissioner only for cause.

(7) Create a new FDA advisory committee on communication with patients and consumers. That committee would be composed of members who represent the interests of patients and consumers.

(8) Require that a "substantial majority" of FDA advisory committees have no significant financial involvement with drug companies.

(9) Five years after a new drug has been approved, the FDA must evaluate all new data on that drug.

*Institute of Medicine, "The Future of Drug Safety: Action Steps for Congress," Report Brief, http://www.iom.edu/CMS/3793/26341/37329/37331.aspx.

## Improving the Clinical-trial Process

Advocates on both sides of the drug-regulation debate have offered proposals aimed at improving the clinical-trial process. Backers of stronger regulation support measures aimed at reducing the pharmaceutical industry's influence over trials. Some, like Dr. Marcia Angell, believe that an independent government agency should oversee trials.

A related issue is the reporting of trial results. An Institute of Medicine panel recommended that most such results be made public. Disclosure would make it easier for other scientists to evaluate them and more difficult for drug companies to suppress unfavorable results. Clifton Leaf of *Fortune* magazine adds that, "when nasty side effects show up years later (and they will—drugs are rarely so specific that they affect only a precise biological target), no one can say that companies knew of the risks in earlier trials and hid them."[97] Reformers such as Angell also propose making trials meaningful by requiring that proposed new drugs be evaluated against a drug already on the market rather than against a placebo.

Those who urge further deregulation contend that the clinical-trial approach, which was developed decades ago to deal with powerful but potentially deadly anti-cancer drugs, has become an unnecessary barrier to bringing new medicines to market. Suggested alternatives include expanding "fast-track" approval programs to all drugs, and allowing drug manufacturers to market drugs while trials are going on—a procedure that is currently used for certain AIDS and cancer drugs. Some believe that the FDA should no longer have a monopoly over drug approval. They propose "farming out" the tasks of overseeing trials and reviewing drug applications to FDA-certified private laboratories. This is the approach followed by European regulators. Professor Richard Epstein explains:

> For the most part, devices are overseen there by "notified bodies," nongovernmental entities sanctioned by government;

and the review of the equivalent of new drug applications
is performed under contract by academics skilled in the
various areas. . . . This arrangement resembles the role of
Underwriters Laboratories and its competitors in setting
standards for and certifying tens of thousands of categories
of consumer products.[98]

Underwriters Laboratories is not only highly regarded, but it has
tested thousands of consumer products, including products that
have the potential to injure or kill people.

The high cost of approval has forced manufacturers to concentrate on drugs aimed at diseases that affect a large number of
patients and require long-term treatment. Some believe that the
government should step in and develop medicines for illnesses
that affect smaller populations. Advocates of a free market are
skeptical of this. Professor Richard Epstein argues that the government lacks the know-how to market the drugs it develops
or to look for new opportunities. Henry Grabowski of Duke
University adds that there are limits to the government's ability to develop drugs. He wrote that "[g]overnment-supported
research gets you to the 20-yard line. . . . By and large, government labs don't do any drug development. The real originator of
90 percent of prescription drugs is private industry."[99] Advocates
of market forces believe that less government involvement, not
more, will make the next generation of medicines a reality.

## Post-approval Monitoring of Drugs

Some members of the medical community, such as Dr. Avorn,
believe that the FDA should have broader authority to regulate
drugs that are already on the market. He wrote:

The first day a new drug is on the market should mark the
start of a systematic ongoing evaluation of how wisely doctors are prescribing it, how thoroughly patients are taking it,

what adverse events it causes in routine care, and (eventually) whether its promised benefits are actually being realized with routine use.[100]

The Institute of Medicine has offered recommendations that would extend the FDA's approach toward proposed new drugs to those already on the market. Those recommendations require action by Congress.

After Vioxx was taken off the market, Senator Charles Grassley, an Iowa Republican, commented: "When the FDA approves a drug, it's considered a 'Good Housekeeping Seal of Approval.' However, what's come to light about Vioxx since September 30 makes people wonder if the FDA has lost its way when it comes to making sure drugs are safe."[101] Advocates of stronger regulation believe that Vioxx should have been withdrawn sooner, and blame both Merck and the FDA for responding too slowly to trial results that linked the drug to adverse reactions. During congressional hearings over the FDA's handling of Vioxx, Dr. David Graham, a scientist who clashed with his superiors over the need for stronger warnings for the drug, told lawmakers: "This culture within the FDA ... views the pharmaceutical industry it is supposed to regulate as its client, over-values the benefits of drugs it approves, and seriously undervalues, disregards, and disrespects drug safety."[102]

Some who favor stronger regulation urge the United States to follow the lead of other English-speaking countries and allow the government to independently evaluate drugs that are on the market. Others, however, believe that the private sector would be more effective in monitoring such drugs. One proposal is to put post-approval evaluation in the hands of a private-sector agency similar to Standard & Poor's, which rates the financial health of companies. Another possibility is to make greater use of patient records to monitor drugs. In the Netherlands, the medical profession has established a database that contains patient

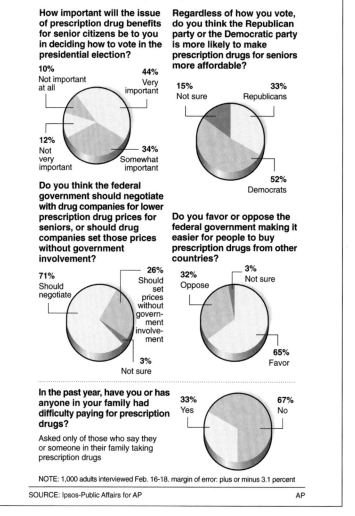

# Prescription drugs an issue in elections

Americans want more done to lower the cost of prescription drugs for seniors. About four out of five Americans say they have someone in their family taking prescription drugs.

**How important will the issue of prescription drug benefits for senior citizens be to you in deciding how to vote in the presidential election?**

- 10% Not important at all
- 44% Very important
- 12% Not very important
- 34% Somewhat important

**Regardless of how you vote, do you think the Republican party or the Democratic party is more likely to make prescription drugs for seniors more affordable?**

- 15% Not sure
- 33% Republicans
- 52% Democrats

**Do you think the federal government should negotiate with drug companies for lower prescription drug prices for seniors, or should drug companies set those prices without government involvement?**

- 71% Should negotiate
- 26% Should set prices without government involvement
- 3% Not sure

**Do you favor or oppose the federal government making it easier for people to buy prescription drugs from other countries?**

- 32% Oppose
- 3% Not sure
- 65% Favor

**In the past year, have you or has anyone in your family had difficulty paying for prescription drugs?**

Asked only of those who say they or someone in their family taking prescription drugs

- 33% Yes
- 67% No

NOTE: 1,000 adults interviewed Feb. 16-18. margin of error: plus or minus 3.1 percent

SOURCE: Ipsos-Public Affairs for AP                                    AP

In the 2004 election cycle, prescription drug prices were an important issue for American voters. In an AP poll—the results of which are shown above—many said that they wanted the government to do more to lower the cost of drugs, especially for senior citizens.

information, which individual doctors can use to identify drugs that might cause adverse reactions in their own patients. In this country, drug reactions are under-reported. The FDA operates a monitoring system called MedWatch, but there is no requirement that health-care personnel use it. By one estimate, only 1 in 10 reactions are reported.

After the Vioxx recall, some in the scientific community accused regulators of approving drugs despite having doubts as to whether they were safe. Dr. Angell believes that one way to prevent the next Vioxx is to require Phase IV trials more often. She explains why these trials are needed:

> Even large, well-designed Phase III trials may not reveal side effects if they are very rare or no one thought to look for them. They may also miss other effects that show up only in patients different from those previously studied. After the drug comes on the market and is used widely in the general population, those properties may be discovered in large Phase IV studies.[103]

Reformers also fault the FDA for not forcing companies to keep their promise to conduct Phase IV trials. The Institute of Medicine has recommended giving the agency power to withdraw approval if the trials are not conducted.

On the other hand, those who favor deregulation criticize the FDA's "all-or-nothing" approach to approval. In their view, if a drug can help some groups of patients, it should remain available, but with limits on who may prescribe it. Robert Goldberg and Peter Pitts of the Manhattan Institute explain:

> Some drugs, such as Vioxx, may cause problems for a small subset of people. Others [sic] drugs, such as thalidomide, may be intolerable for broad populations but useful in subpopulations; thalidomide has been widely used to treat certain cancers. Instead of taking "bad" drugs off the market, or

plastering them with interminable warning labels, regulators and industry should work together to develop personalized medicines that can better ensure that people who can safely benefit from these drugs get them and that those who are [at] risk avoid them.[104]

# The Pharmaceutical Industry's Advertising Guidelines

In October 2005, the Pharmaceutical Research and Manufacturers of America (PhRMA) adopted a set of guidelines* governing direct-to-consumer (DTC) advertising. These guidelines do not have the force of law, and there are no penalties for violating them. Most drug companies, however, have agreed to follow them.

PhRMA maintains that direct-to-consumer advertising should remain legal. It states:

"A strong empirical record demonstrates that DTC communications about prescription medicines serve the public health by:

- Increasing awareness about diseases;

- Educating patients about treatment options;

- Motivating patients to contact their physicians and engage in a dialogue about health concerns;

- Increasing the likelihood that patients will receive appropriate care for conditions that are frequently under-diagnosed and under-treated; and

- Encouraging compliance with prescription drug treatment regimens."

PhRMA's guidelines include the following provisions:

(1) In general, direct-to-consumer advertising should meet FDA standards—namely, that it be accurate and not misleading, that claims be supported by substantial evidence, that risks and benefits be given a balanced presentation, and that content be consistent with FDA-approved labeling.

## Countering Drug Company Influence

Many observers contend that drug companies have too much influence over the entire health-care system. They warn that drug company money can compromise the independence of scientists and even influence how doctors treat their patients. In January

(2) Companies should submit new television advertisements to the FDA before airing them. The law currently requires companies to submit their advertisements at the time they first air.

(3) Advertisements should responsibly educate the consumer about the drug and about the condition for which it may be prescribed. They should encourage communications between patients and their doctors. When appropriate, they should inform consumers of alternatives to medication, such as diet and lifestyle changes.

(4) Advertisements should clearly identify prescription drugs as such, and identify the conditions for which the drug has been approved.

(5) Advertisements should identify the major risks associated with the drug, and provide a balanced presentation of its benefits and risks in clear and understandable language.

(6) Advertisements should respect the seriousness of the drug being advertised and the medical condition that it is intended to treat.

(7) Companies should tailor advertisements to "age-appropriate" audiences.

(8) If a company discovers that the drug presents a safety risk, it should change its advertising or stop it altogether.

(9) Before launching an advertising campaign, drug companies should spend an appropriate amount of time educating doctors about the new drug. How much time is "appropriate" depends on the drug's risks and how much the medical community knows about the condition being treated.

(10) Companies are encouraged to promote health and disease awareness and make the public aware of help for the uninsured and underinsured.

*Pharmaceutical Research and Manufacturers of America, "PhRMA Guiding Principles: Direct to Consumer Advertisements About Prescription Medicines," http://www.phrma .org/files/DTCGuidingprinciples.pdf.

2006, the authors of an article in the *Journal of the American Medical Association* called for an end to drug company sponsorship of continuing medical education and "ghost-writing" of journal articles, and even recommended a ban on the doctors accepting free samples from drug company representatives.

Some, however, believe that the influence of drug company money has been exaggerated. A *Wall Street Journal* editorial argued that "the most qualified scientists and doctors have substantial sources of private income," thus making them less susceptible to drug companies' influence. It also cited "a study by the Naderite Public Citizen group that failed to find one instance of a panel recommendation that would have changed if allegedly conflicted members had been excluded."[105]

## Regulation of Drug Advertising

Aside from the United States, direct-to-consumer drug advertising is allowed in only one other Western country—New Zealand—and that country is reconsidering the policy. Consumer advocates cite Vioxx as the worst example of irresponsible drug promotion. "From the beginning, everyone, including the company, agreed that not everybody ought to be getting Vioxx," said Helen Darling, president of the National Business Group on Health, an organization of large employers. "But the ads implied there was a widespread need for it."[106] In 2005, PhRMA reacted to bad post-Vioxx publicity by adopting a set of advertising guidelines. Some advocates and lawmakers believe that the guidelines do not go far enough. For example, they set out no fixed waiting period before a new drug may be advertised; they merely call on companies to wait an "appropriate time."

## The Future of Deregulation

Some advocates of deregulation consider the "effectiveness" requirement unnecessary. Doug Bandow of the Cato Institute explains that if no such requirement existed, "drug companies still would have no incentive to sell ineffective products, doctors would have no incentive to prescribe them, and patients would have no incentive to buy them."[107] Epstein insists that market forces work: "This market has serious players on both sides; if the various physicians, insurers, and pharmaceutical-benefit managers choose the new product over the old one, it is hard to attack this decision on the ground that they are ill-informed or have no bargaining power."[108]

Others favor more sweeping forms of deregulation. One proposal involves doing away entirely with the requirement of FDA approval and relying instead on market forces to combat inferior drugs. Another is to allow over-the-counter sales of a wide variety of drugs that currently require a prescription. Some even support the legalization of Internet pharmacies. They argue that consumers are more likely to go online to buy popular drugs designed to treat common problems, but will consult a doctor if they suffer from a serious medical condition.

But advocates of strong regulation believe that without the help of a doctor or pharmacist, patients run the risk of adverse reactions due to an overdose or interaction with other substances. They also warn that doing away with the requirement of a face-to-face transaction could result in underage sales and expose buyers to counterfeit and adulterated drugs.

## Summary

The FDA will continue to play a significant role in regulating drugs. The renewal of the Prescription Drug User Fee Act in 2007 will force Congress to address a series of broader controversies relating to drug regulation. One issue involves how best to prove that drugs are safe and effective. Some advocates favor stricter requirements for clinical trials, while others believe that market forces are the best guarantee of quality. Other issues include whether closer post-approval monitoring is necessary, whether drug advertising should come under closer regulation, and what steps should be taken to limit the pharmaceutical industry's influence over health care. Some believe that it is time to do away with many, if not most, restrictions on access to drugs—including the requirement of a prescription.

# ///////// NOTES

### Introduction: Drug Regulation in America

1 Roderick E. McGrew, *Encyclopedia of Medical History* (New York: McGraw-Hill Book Company, 1985), p. 251.

2 Philip J. Hilts, *Protecting America's Health: The FDA, Business, and One Hundred Years of Regulation* (New York: Alfred A. Knopf, 2003), p. 41.

3 McGrew, *Encyclopedia of Medical History*, p. 256.

4 Hilts, *Protecting America's Health*, p. 55.

5 *Ibid*, p. 107.

6 Public Law 87-781, §102(c).

7 Hilts, *Protecting America's Health*, p. 160.

8 David F. Musto, *The American Disease: Origins of Narcotic Control* (New York: Oxford University Press, 1987), p. 11.

9 Title II of Public Law 91-513, the Comprehensive Drug Abuse Prevention and Control Act; 21 USC §801 et seq.

### Point: Drug Companies' Business Practices Endanger Americans

10 Hilts, *Protecting America's Health*, p. 307–308.

11 Jacky Law, *Big Pharma: Exposing the Global Healthcare Agenda* (New York: Carroll & Graf Publishers, 2006), p. 18.

12 Marcia Angell, M.D., *The Truth About Drug Companies: How They Deceive Us and What to Do About It* (New York: Random House, 2004), p. 75.

13 *Ibid.*, p. 91.

14 Hilts, *Protecting America's Health*, p. 194.

15 Law, *Big Pharma*, p. 13.

16 *Ibid.* p. 46.

17 Angell, *The Truth About Drug Companies*, p. 95.

18 Lawrence Altman, "For Science's Gatekeepers, a Credibility Gap," *New York Times*. May 2, 2006.

19 W. John Thomas, "The Vioxx Story: Would It Have Ended Differently in the European Union?" *American Journal of Law & Medicine*. 32 no. 2–3 (2006): p. 370.

20 Jerry Avorn, M.D., *Powerful Medicines: The Benefits, Risks, and Costs of Prescription Drugs* (New York: Alfred A. Knopf, 2004), p. 374.

21 Law, *Big Pharma*, p. 95.

22 "Industry Totals: Pharmaceuticals/Health Products," opensecrets.org: Your Guide to the Money in U.S. Elections. http://opensecrets.org/industries/indus.asp?Ind=H04.

23 Law, *Big Pharma*, p. 169–170.

24 *Ibid.*, p.170.

25 Hilts, *Protecting America's Health*, p. 342.

26 Angell, *The Truth About Drug Companies*, p. 170–171.

27 Greg Critser, *Generation Rx: How Prescription Drugs are Altering American Lives, Minds, and Bodies* (Boston: Houghton Mifflin Company, 2005), p. 216.

### Counterpoint: Regulation Is More Dangerous Than Drug Side Effects

28 Andrew Pollack, "New Sense of Caution at F.D.A.," *New York Times*. September 29, 2006.

29 Avorn, *Powerful Medicines*, p. 141.

30 *Ibid.*, p. 122–123.

31 Julie Scelfo, "'Opportunity for Improvement': FDA Defends Its Drug Safety Record," *Newsweek*. October 12, 2006.

32 Clifton Leaf, "Deadly Caution: How Our National Obsession with Drug Safety Is Killing People—And What We Can Do about It," *Fortune*. February 20, 2006.

33 Richard A. Epstein, *Overdose: How Excessive Government Regulation Stifles Pharmaceutical Innovation* (New Haven, Conn.: Yale University Press, 2006) p. 116.

34 Rochelle Lee, "FDA and Drug Safety: New Tufts Study Challenges Critics of the Prescription Drug User Fee Act," *Journal of Law, Medicine and Ethics* 34, no. 1 (Spring 2006): 131.

35 Hilts, *Protecting America's Health*, p. 235.

36 Editorial, "Faster FDA Cures," *Wall Street Journal*. October 13, 2006.

37 Critser, *Generation Rx*, p. 148.

38 Leaf, "Deadly Caution."

39 Doug Bandow, *Demonizing Drugmakers: The Political Assault on the Pharmaceutical Industry*, Cato Institute Policy Analysis Paper No. 475 (Washington, D.C.: Cato Institute, 2003), p. 33.

40 Alex Berenson, "A Cancer Drug's Big Price is Cause for Concern," *New York Times*. March 12, 2006.

**Point: Drug Prices Are Unreasonably High**

41 Public Citizen, Congress Watch, "2002 Drug Industry Profits: Hefty Pharmaceutical Company Margins Dwarf Other Industries," p. 2, http://www.citizen.org/ congress/reform/drug_industry/r_d/ articles.cfm?ID=9923.

42 Families USA, The Choice: Health Care for People or Drug Industry Profits," p. 11, http://www.familiesusa.org/ resources/publications/reports/ the-choice.html.

43 Prescription Access Litigation Project, "Letter to the Federal Trade Commission, 'Re: FTC Project No. P062105: Authorized Generic Drug Study,' Community Catalyst, http://www .communitycatalyst.org/resource .php?base_id=1054.

44 Public Citizen, "Would Lower Prescription Drug Prices Curb Drug Company Research & Development?" http://www .citizen.org/congress/reform/drug_ industry/r_d/articles.cfm?ID=7909.

45 Critser, *Generation Rx*, p. 132.

46 Angell, *The Truth About Drug Companies*, p. 183.

47 John Carreyrou, "Inside Abbott's Tactics to Protect AIDS Drug," *Wall Street Journal*. January 3, 2007.

48 Public Citizen, "Would Lower Prescription Drug Prices Curb Drug Company Research & Development?"

49 Berenson, "A Cancer Drug's Big Price is Cause for Concern."

50 Marcia Angell and Arnold S. Relman, op-ed, "Prescription for Profit," *Washington Post*, June 20, 2001.

**Counterpoint: Drugs Are Fairly Priced**

51 John A. Vernon, Rexford E. Santerre, and Carmelo Giacotto, "Are Drug Price Controls Good for Your Health?" Manhattan Institute for Public Policy Research Medical Progress Report No. 1., http://www.manhattan-institute.org/ html/mpr_01.htm.

52 Avorn, *Powerful Medicines*, p. 221–222.

53 Pharmaceutical Research and Manufacturers of America, "What Goes Into the Cost of Prescription Drugs? . . . And Other Questions About Your Medicines," p. 6, http://www.phrma.org/files/Cost_ of_Prescription_Drugs.pdf. [pdf].

54 Ibid.

55 *Wall Street Journal*, "Little Big Pharma," December 6, 2006.

56 Richard A. Epstein, "What's Good for Pharma Is Good for America," *Boston Globe*. December 3, 2006.

57 Epstein, *Overdose*, p. 56.

58 Bandow, *Demonizing Drugmakers*, p. 18.

59 *Ibid.*, p. 12.

60 Milton Friedman, et al., "Economists Warn of Dangers of Drug Importation, Price Controls," Heartland Institute, http://www.heartland.org/Article .cfm?artId=14308.

61 Avorn, *Powerful Medicines*, p. 237.

62 Alain Enthoven and Kyna Fong, op-ed, "Pelosi on Drugs," *Wall Street Journal*. November 13, 2006.

63 Epstein, *Overdose*, p. 73.

**Point: Drugs Should Not Be Marketed Like Other Products**

64 Hilts, *Protecting America's Health*, p. 323.

65 *Ibid.*, p. 141.

66 Critser, *Generation Rx*, p. 133. (emphasis original)

67 *Ibid.*, p. 113.

68 Hilts, *Protecting America's Health*, p. 106–107.

69 Angell, *The Truth About Drug Companies*, p. 35.

70 *Ibid*, p. 133.

# NOTES

71 *Virginia State Board of Pharmacy v. Virginia Citizens Consumer Council*, 425 U.S. 748, 788-89 (1976) (Rehnquist, J., dissenting).

72 Critser, *Generation Rx*, p. 52.

73 *Ibid*, p. 106.

74 Avorn, *Powerful Medicines*, p. 289.

75 Hilts, *Protecting America's Health*, p. xi.

76 *Ibid*, p. 281.

77 Jerome Groopman, op-ed, "No Alternative," *Wall Street Journal*. August 8, 2006.

78 *Ibid*.

## Counterpoint: A Free Market in Drugs Serves the Public

79 *Virginia State Board of Pharmacy v. Virginia Citizens Consumer Council*, 425 U.S. 748, 765 (1976).

80 Epstein, *Overdose*, p. 146.

81 Ronald F. White, "Direct-to-Consumer Advertising and the Demise of the Ideal Model of Health Care," *Independent Review*, 11, no. 2 (Fall 2006): 233.

82 Pharmaceutical Research and Manufacturers of America, "What Goes Into the Cost of Prescription Drugs?"

83 Richard O. Dolinar, "The DTC Double Standard," *Pharmaceutical Representative* (November 1, 2004), http://downloads.heartland.org/17224.pdf. [pdf].

84 *Ibid*.

85 *Wall Street Journal*, "Little Big Pharma."

86 Pharmaceutical Research and Manufacturers Association, "PhRMA Guiding Principles: Direct to Consumer Advertisements About Prescription Medicines," http://www.phrma.org/principles_and_guidelines.

87 Epstein, "What's Good for Pharma Is Good for America."

88 *Ibid*.

89 Bandow, *Demonizing Drugmakers*, p. 7.

90 Angell, *The Truth About Drug Companies*, p. 169.

91 White, "Direct-to-Consumer Advertising and the Demise of the Ideal Model of Health Care."

92 Thomas Szasz, *Our Right to Drugs* (New York: Praeger Publishers, 1992), p. 42 (emphasis original).

93 *Webb v. United States*, 249 U.S. 96, 99-100 (1919).

## Conclusion: Drug Regulation in the Twenty-first Century

94 Avorn, *Powerful Medicines*, p. 418.

95 Hilts, *Protecting America's Health*, p. 304.

96 *Ibid.*, p. xv.

97 Leaf, "Deadly Caution."

98 Epstein, *Overdose*, p. 128–129.

99 Bandow, *Demonizing Drugmakers*, p. 9.

100 Avorn, *Powerful Medicines*, p. 383–384.

101 Senate Finance Committee Hearing, opening statement by Chairman Charles Grassley, on November 18, 2004, "FDA, Merck and Vioxx: Putting Patient Safety First?"

102 Thomas, "The Vioxx Story."

103 Angell, *The Truth About Drug Companies*, p. 162.

104 Robert Goldberg and Peter Pitts, "Prescription for Progress: The Critical Path to Drug Development: A Working Paper of the 21st Century FDA Task Force," p. 1–2, Manhattan Institute, http://www.manhattan-institute.org/html/fda_task_1.htm.

105 *Wall Street Journal*, "Faster FDA Cures," October 13, 2006.

106 Milt Freudenheim, "Showdown Looms in Congress Over Drug Advertising on TV," *New York Times*. January 22, 2007.

107 Bandow, *Demonizing Drugmakers*, p. 33.

108 Epstein, *Overdose*, p. 63.

## Books and Articles

Angell, Marcia, M.D. *The Truth About Drug Companies: How They Deceive Us and What to Do About It.* New York: Random House, 2004.

Avorn, Jerry, M.D. *Powerful Medicines: The Benefits, Risks, and Costs of Prescription Drugs.* New York: Alfred A. Knopf, 2004.

Bandow, Doug. *Demonizing Drugmakers: The Political Assault on the Pharmaceutical Industry.* Cato Institute Policy Analysis Paper No. 475. Washington, D.C.: Cato Institute, 2003.

Critser, Greg. *Generation Rx: How Prescription Drugs are Altering American Lives, Minds, and Bodies.* Boston: Houghton Mifflin Company, 2005.

Epstein, Richard A. *Overdose: How Excessive Government Regulation Stifles Pharmaceutical Innovation.* New Haven, Conn.: Yale University Press, 2006.

Hilts, Philip J. *Protecting America's Health: The FDA, Business, and One Hundred Years of Regulation.* New York: Alfred A. Knopf, 2003.

Law, Jacky. *Big Pharma: Exposing the Global Healthcare Agenda.* New York: Carroll & Graf Publishers, 2006.

## Web Sites

### AARP

*www.aarp.org*

The AARP represents tens of millions of older Americans. It favors legislation that would authorize the Medicare program to negotiate with drug companies to obtain lower prices and that would allow Americans to import medication from other countries.

### The American Medical Association

*www.ama-assn.org*

The AMA is the nation's largest organization of medical doctors. Its objective is to promote the interests of the medical profession. It publishes the authoritative *Journal of the American Medical Association,* which presents the findings of medical and scientific studies as well as the views of leaders of the profession.

### The Cato Institute

*www.cato.org*

The Cato Institute is an organization that favors "individual liberty, limited government, free markets, and peace." It blames regulation for driving up the cost of health care.

### The Council for Responsible Nutrition

*www.crnusa.org*

The CRN is the trade association of companies that manufacture and supply vitamins and other nutritional supplements. The council favors self-regulation as

an alternative to stronger government regulation, and has drawn up a code of ethics for its members.

## Families USA

*www.familiesusa.org*
Families USA is an advocacy group with the goal of promoting high-quality, affordable medical care for all Americans. It favors expansion of government health-care programs and is critical of the pharmaceutical industry.

## The Manhattan Institute

*www.manhattan-institute.org*
The Manhattan Institute is a research and advocacy organization that favors a market-based approach. It supports the Critical Path Initiative, which it hopes will use advances in genetics and other fields to develop "personalized medicine."

## The National Center for Policy Analysis

*www.ncpa.org*
The NCPA is a research and advocacy organization that favors free-market solutions. One of the center's initiatives is "consumer-driven" health care (cdhc .ncpa.org).

## The Pharmaceutical Research and Manufacturers of America (PhRMA)

*www.phrma.org*
PhRMA is a trade association that advocates the interests of the nation's drug makers. PhRMA favors direct-to-consumer advertising and strong protection of drug patents, and opposes price controls as well as direct price negotiation between government and drug manufacturers.

## Public Citizen

*www.citizen.org*
An advocacy organization founded by Ralph Nader, Public Citizen represents the interests of consumers on a variety of public health and safety issues. One of its aims is ensuring safe and affordable prescription drugs. Its "Worst Pills" Web site (www.worstpills.org) alerts consumers to unsafe and overpriced medication.

## The Tufts Center for the Study of Drug Development

*csdd.tufts.edu*
The Center for the Study of Drug Development is a research center affiliated with Tufts University. It advocates regulatory approaches that will make the drug approval process less time-consuming and expensive.

## U.S. Food and Drug Administration

*www.fda.gov*
The FDA was created in 1927 and is now an administration within the U.S. Department of Health and Human Services. The FDA is responsible for ensuring the safety of the nation's food supply, prescription and non-prescription drugs, and medical devices. It enforces the "safe and effective" requirement for proposed new drugs.

## Cases

**Food and Drug Administration v. Brown & Williamson Tobacco Corporation,** 529 U.S. 120 (2000).
Held that the FDA lacked authority to regulate nicotine as a drug because Congress had made it clear that it would be in charge of regulating the marketing of tobacco.

**Gonzalez v. Raich,** 545 U.S. 1 (2005).
Held that the federal Controlled Substances Act, which banned the use of medical marijuana, invalidated state laws that permitted doctors to prescribe the drug to seriously ill patients.

**Pharmaceutical Research and Manufacturers of America v. Walsh,** 538 U.S. 644 (2003).
Refused to halt a program under which the state of Maine used its bargaining power under Medicaid to obtain lower drug prices for state residents who lacked health insurance.

**United States v. Rutherford,** 442 U.S. 544 (1979).
Unanimously upheld the FDA's authority to keep unproven drugs off the market, even for patients who have been diagnosed as terminally ill with cancer.

**Virginia State Board of Pharmacy v. Virginia Citizens Consumer Council,** 425 U.S. 748 (1976).
Struck down a state law banning pharmacists from advertising the price of prescription drugs on the grounds that such a ban violated the First Amendment's right of "commercial free speech."

## Provisions of the Constitution

### Article I, §8, the Commerce Clause
Provides that Congress has the power to "make all Laws which shall be necessary and proper for carrying into Execution" its authority to "regulate Commerce with foreign Nations, and among the several States."

### Article VI, Paragraph 2, the Supremacy Clause
Provides that "This Constitution, and the Laws of the United States which shall be made in Pursuance thereof; and all Treaties made, or which shall be made, under the authority of the United States, shall be the supreme Law of the land."

### The First Amendment
Provides that "Congress shall make no law . . . abridging the freedom of speech, or of the press; or the right of the people peaceably to assemble, and to petition the Government for a redress of grievances."

## Other Legal Materials

### The Controlled Substances Act
Codified as Title 21, Sections 801, and following of the United States Code. It took effect in 1970. The act recodified the nation's drug laws, and created five

schedules of controlled substances with varying levels of restrictions as to who may dispense or use them. Federal narcotics regulation began with the Harrison Narcotics Act, which was passed in 1917. Later acts of Congress extended federal drug control to a wider range of drugs.

### The Food, Drug and Cosmetic Act

Codified as Title 21, Sections 301, and following of the United States Code. It governs prescription and non-prescription drugs. The first federal law in this area was the Pure Food and Drug Act of 1906, which barred adulterated and misbranded drugs from interstate commerce. Legislation passed in 1938 required manufacturers to provide evidence that a drug was safe. The Kefauver Amendment, passed in 1962, required that a drug be effective as well as safe, and put the burden of proof on the drug's manufacturer.

### The Prescription Drug User Fee Act

First passed in 1992, it offers an accelerated FDA approval schedule for a proposed new drug in exchange for the manufacturer paying the agency a fee. The act comes up for renewal in 2007. The FDA Modernization Act of 1997 contains a number of provisions aimed at streamlining the approval process. Both acts amended various provisions of the Food, Drug and Cosmetic Act.

## Terms and Concepts

adverse reaction

"black box" warning

"blockbuster" drug

clinical trials

Commerce Clause

conflict of interest

continuing medical education

Controlled Substances Act

deregulation

dietary supplement

direct-to-consumer advertising

drug recall

Food and Drug Administration

generic drug

importation

Kefauver Amendment

Medicaid

Medicare Part D

"me-too" drug

"off-label"

over-the-counter

patent

pharmacy

Phase IV

pre-emption

price controls

Pure Food and Drug Act

prescription drug

"safe and effective"

scientific method

self-medication

side effects

user fee

## APPENDIX

### Beginning Legal Research

The goal of POINT/COUNTERPOINT is not only to provide the reader with an introduction to a controversial issue affecting society, but also to encourage the reader to explore the issue more fully. This appendix, then, is meant to serve as a guide to the reader in researching the current state of the law as well as exploring some of the public-policy arguments as to why existing laws should be changed or new laws are needed.

Like many types of research, legal research has become much faster and more accessible with the invention of the Internet. This appendix discusses some of the best starting points, but of course "surfing the Net" will uncover endless additional sources of information—some more reliable than others. Some important sources of law are not yet available on the Internet, but these can generally be found at the larger public and university libraries. Librarians usually are happy to point patrons in the right direction.

The most important source of law in the United States is the Constitution. Originally enacted in 1787, the Constitution outlines the structure of our federal government and sets limits on the types of laws that the federal government and state governments can pass. Through the centuries, a number of amendments have been added to or changed in the Constitution, most notably the first ten amendments, known collectively as the Bill of Rights, which guarantee important civil liberties. Each state also has its own constitution, many of which are similar to the U.S. Constitution. It is important to be familiar with the U.S. Constitution because so many of our laws are affected by its requirements. State constitutions often provide protections of individual rights that are even stronger than those set forth in the U.S. Constitution.

Within the guidelines of the U.S. Constitution, Congress—both the House of Representatives and the Senate—passes bills that are either vetoed or signed into law by the president. After the passage of the law, it becomes part of the United States Code, which is the official compilation of federal laws. The state legislatures use a similar process, in which bills become law when signed by the state's governor. Each state has its own official set of laws, some of which are published by the state and some of which are published by commercial publishers. The U.S. Code and the state codes are an important source of legal research; generally, legislators make efforts to make the language of the law as clear as possible.

However, reading the text of a federal or state law generally provides only part of the picture. In the American system of government, after the

**112**

legislature passes laws and the executive (U.S. president or state governor) signs them, it is up to the judicial branch of the government, the court system, to interpret the laws and decide whether they violate any provision of the Constitution. At the state level, each state's supreme court has the ultimate authority in determining what a law means and whether or not it violates the state constitution. However, the federal courts—headed by the U.S. Supreme Court—can review state laws and court decisions to determine whether they violate federal laws or the U.S. Constitution. For example, a state court may find that a particular criminal law is valid under the state's constitution, but a federal court may then review the state court's decision and determine that the law is invalid under the U.S. Constitution.

It is important, then, to read court decisions when doing legal research. The Constitution uses language that is intentionally very general—for example, prohibiting "unreasonable searches and seizures" by the police—and court cases often provide more guidance. For example, the U.S. Supreme Court's 2001 decision in *Kyllo* v. *United States* held that scanning the outside of a person's house using a heat sensor to determine whether the person is growing marijuana is unreasonable—*if* it is done without a search warrant secured from a judge. Supreme Court decisions provide the most definitive explanation of the law of the land, and it is therefore important to include these in research. Often, when the Supreme Court has not decided a case on a particular issue, a decision by a federal appeals court or a state supreme court can provide guidance; but just as laws and constitutions can vary from state to state, so can federal courts be split on a particular interpretation of federal law or the U.S. Constitution. For example, federal appeals courts in Louisiana and California may reach opposite conclusions in similar cases.

Lawyers and courts refer to statutes and court decisions through a formal system of citations. Use of these citations reveals which court made the decision (or which legislature passed the statute) and when and enables the reader to locate the statute or court case quickly in a law library. For example, the legendary Supreme Court case *Brown* v. *Board of Education* has the legal citation 347 U.S. 483 (1954). At a law library, this 1954 decision can be found on page 483 of volume 347 of the U.S. Reports, the official collection of the Supreme Court's decisions. Citations can also be helpful in locating court cases on the Internet.

Understanding the current state of the law leads only to a partial understanding of the issues covered by the POINT/COUNTERPOINT series. For a fuller understanding of the issues, it is necessary to look at public-policy arguments that the current state of the law is not adequately addressing the issue.

Many groups lobby for new legislation or changes to existing legislation; the National Rifle Association (NRA), for example, lobbies Congress and the state legislatures constantly to make existing gun control laws less restrictive and not to pass additional laws. The NRA and other groups dedicated to various causes might also intervene in pending court cases: a group such as Planned Parenthood might file a brief *amicus curiae* (as "a friend of the court")—called an "amicus brief"—in a lawsuit that could affect abortion rights. Interest groups also use the media to influence public opinion, issuing press releases and frequently appearing in interviews on news programs and talk shows. The books in POINT/COUNTERPOINT list some of the interest groups that are active in the issue at hand, but in each case there are countless other groups working at the local, state, and national levels. It is important to read everything with a critical eye, for sometimes interest groups present information in a way that can be read only to their advantage. The informed reader must always look for bias.

Finding sources of legal information on the Internet is relatively simple thanks to "portal" sites such as FindLaw (*www.findlaw.com*), which provides access to a variety of constitutions, statutes, court opinions, law review articles, news articles, and other resources—including all Supreme Court decisions issued since 1893. Other useful sources of information include the U.S. Government Printing Office (*www.gpo.gov*), which contains a complete copy of the U.S. Code, and the Library of Congress's THOMAS system (*thomas.loc.gov*), which offers access to bills pending before Congress as well as recently passed laws. Of course, the Internet changes every second of every day, so it is best to do some independent searching. Most cases, studies, and opinions that are cited or referred to in public debate can be found online—and *everything* can be found in one library or another.

The Internet can provide a basic understanding of most important legal issues, but not all sources can be found there. To find some documents it is necessary to visit the law library of a university or a public law library; some cities have public law libraries, and many library systems keep legal documents at the main branch. On the following page are some common citation forms.

**PAUL RUSCHMANN, J.D.,** is a legal analyst and writer based in Canton, Michigan. He received his undergraduate degree from the University of Notre Dame and his law degree from the University of Michigan. He is a member of the State Bar of Michigan. His areas of specialization include legislation, public safety, traffic and transportation, and trade regulation. He is also the author of eight other titles in the POINT/COUNTERPOINT series, including *The War on Terror, The FCC and Regulating Indecency, Tort Reform, Media Bias,* and *Miranda Rights.* He can be found online at *www.PaulRuschmann.com* and *www.BlueLionMedia.com.*

**ALAN MARZILLI, M.A., J.D.,** lives in Washington, D.C., and is a program associate with Advocates for Human Potential, Inc., a research and consulting firm based in Sudbury, Mass., and Albany, N.Y. He primarily works on developing training and educational materials for agencies of the federal government on topics such as housing, mental health policy, employment, and transportation. He has spoken on mental health issues in 30 states, the District of Columbia, and Puerto Rico; his work has included training mental health administrators, nonprofit management and staff, and people with mental illnesses and their families on a wide variety of topics, including effective advocacy, community-based mental health services, and housing. Marzilli has written several handbooks and training curricula that are used nationally and as far away as the U.S. territory of Guam. Additionally, he managed statewide and national mental health advocacy programs and worked for several public interest lobbying organizations while studying law at Georgetown University. Marzilli has written more than a dozen books, including numerous titles in the POINT/COUNTERPOINT series.